CHILDREN OF THE THIRTIES

Edited by
ROY LEWIS

Published in 2017 by FeedARead.com Publishing

Copyright © Roy Lewis 2017.

First Edition

The author has asserted their moral right under the Copyright, Designs and Patents Act, 1988, to be identified as the author of this work.

All Rights reserved. No part of this publication may be reproduced, copied, stored in a retrieval system, or transmitted, in any form or by any means, without the prior written consent of the copyright holder, nor be otherwise circulated in any form of binding or cover other than that in which it is published and without a similar condition being imposed on the subsequent purchaser.

A CIP catalogue record for this title is available from the British Library.

Photographs on pages 17,57,189 and 247 courtesy of Rhondda Archives

CONTRIBUTORS

Ken Wilkins   7

Gwynfryn Evans   51

Dewi Griffiths   87

Roy Lewis   111

Leighton Brunt   161

Roy Lewis, Keith Lewis, Ken Wilkins and Brian Roberts

INTRODUCTION

WE WERE A SMALL group of close friends brought up in the working class environment of Ton Pentre, in the Rhondda Valley. We were all sons of men who worked, or had worked in the pits. By modern standards we lived among terraced streets in an environment close to poverty levels, but life was simpler then. But we were certainly part of a world that has long since vanished.

We were naturally Rhondda- focused and Rhondda- bound as youngsters, but life turned out to be remarkably diverse for us: individually we had later very different, wide-ranging experiences. Only one of us remained in the Rhondda, carving out an impressive career locally and internationally. The rest of us made very different ways in the world beyond.

We were never in any sense a club, or gang: the group was neither exclusive nor closed, varied in size between five and eight as occasional acquaintances drifted into our orbit for limited periods. We began to coalesce about 1947 drawn together by environment and common interests, particularly a love of music, film and rugby. By 1951 the core group had dispersed to set out on surprisingly varied routes to eventual success: one gained fame as an international sports star, while another enjoyed a glittering career in BBC radio and television. Others were on entirely different routes: leading schools abroad, working in the nuclear industry or writing crime novels.

The last occasion we met as a group was at the annual Bindle's Night Club dance in Barry, along with our girl friends, in 1954. The group was missing Gwyn Evans and Keith Lewis: both had married by then. But as individuals we kept in touch over the years, two or three of us occasionally meeting in the Rhondda, talking over old times, reminiscing. Of course, there was one important thing we had in common—we all attended grammar schools: Porth County, Porth Secondary, Pentre Secondary.

The grammar schools have been a political football for decades, decried as catering for a privileged few but for us, the sons of pitmen, they provided a lifeline and escape from the traditional opportunities in the Rhondda—typically, a dark, grimy life working underground. Instead, members of our small group were given an educational grounding which encouraged us to launch into careers that were denied to our parents and indeed would have been unimaginable to our forbears: forensic scientist, consultant anaesthetist, chief executive, BBC radio and television producer, headmaster, chartered surveyor, college principal and writer of crime novels. Without doubt we all owed much to the education we were given in the grammar schools, even depleted of staff as they were during the Second World War. They gave us a chance which had been denied to previous generations.

But under what conditions did we grow up, and how were our lives shaped by our experiences? These are our stories. These are our voices.

KEN WILKINS

I WAS BORN AT 12 Birchgrove Street, Porth, Rhondda on August 8 1931 in the house in which my mother was born and in which her parents had lived and died. My grandparents had moved to Porth from Carmarthenshire in the 1890's and had brought six children into the world, burying four of them as infants. Only my mother, Morfydd, and her elder sister, Mary, survived the hardships of early twentieth century Rhondda.

Birchgrove was a terrace which climbed steeply, along the side of a hill. Opposite the terrace was a steep slope with an uninterrupted view of Ynyshir and the point at which the two Rhondda valleys divide into the Fach and the Fawr. I was told I arrived on a rainy night and the doctor came by pony and trap to see me safely into the world.

In 1931 my father, Brynmor, was working as a colliery hitcher in the Cymmer pit in Porth, having returned to the Rhondda after serving for several years in the Royal Horse Artillery regiment. He was from Llwyncelyn on the far side of Porth, and his home overlooked Trehafod and the Lewis Merthyr colliery where he, his father and brother Ollie had worked.

The Wilkins' ancestors had moved to Caerphilly from Bristol in the 1790's and then to Pontypridd but by 1902 some had migrated to Porth. By contrast, my father's mother was a Llewellyn from Treherbert whose family can be traced to Kenfig in the 17th century.

The Thirties

My mother's Uncle John, a gentle bachelor who gave me much

attention, lived with us. By 1933 my father was unemployed, and like thousands of other pitmen he was reduced to drawing his dole money of 24/6d each week. He gave this to my mother and she returned to him enough money to buy a packet of five Woodbine cigarettes which would last him the week; as for me 2d was put aside to buy a bar of toffee each day costing one farthing.

My father's sister, Ivy, had married a Cardiganshire man, Tom Thomas He worked in the pit but also rented Rhiw y Uchain farm above Trehafod. There my cousin Dewi was born in 1929. Occasionally my father and his brother Oliver would assist Tom and in return received milk, potatoes and whatever else the farm could provide. Ethel, my father's eldest sister, had married another Cardiganshire man, Tom James, who years later would tell me of scrapes and chases with police as he and other men scavenged for coal on the tips during those Depression years

As unemployment bit deeper so families started to move from the Rhondda.

My aunts Ivy and Ethel and their husbands were the first to leave for London, and they rented shops/dairies in the East End –coming from a farming background, milk was something they knew about. One branch of the family moved to Bridgwater, Somerset. Aunt Ivy soon wrote asking my mother to come lend a hand in what was a busy shop. A few weeks later my mother persuaded my father to join her to open their own shop.

Evidence of entrepreneurship in the Wilkins family!

London Interlude

The premises my parents leased in Stepney consisted of was a small corner shop at 48 Eastfield Street, near the busy Commercial Road. Much of its trade came from the local dockers and their families Shop doors opened at six in the morning six days of the week to serve them. The living quarters were tiny consisting of one room behind the shop and two bedrooms above - the single downstairs room also served as a kitchen. In the small outside yard were two doors, one to a coal cupboard and the other to the toilet.

I attended Hayley Street infants school and on Sundays I went to Sunday School at the Edinburgh Castle Mission which was across "the cut" (Grand Union Canal) and near my aunt's dairy and shop in Apostle's Road, Bow. I played in the nearby park and attended the Troxy cinema on Saturdays, clutching a clean jam jar, the entrance fee for the children's morning matinee usually including serials such as *Buck Rogers* and *Hopalong Cassidy*.

At the nearby street market we would watch live eels being chopped before being cooked and turned into jellied eels. A dairy in a nearby street kept a cow in a byre at the rear of the shop to provide fresh milk to the customers; we would watch the milking, and be there again when the cow was replaced by another fresh from the countryside.

The East End was home to a large Jewish population. The fascist Oswald Moseley and his Blackshirts held meetings in the area and on one occasion a meeting took place outside our shop which ended in a fierce fight between the two factions. But a more cheerful, annual event in our street was at hop-picking time when many Easterners packed their belongings onto lorries and headed for the Kent hop fields for the picking season.

In mid-1939 my cousin Dewi and I were sent to Porth as evacuees, to live with relatives at 84 Leslie Terrace, Llwyncelyn until such time that we could be re-united with our parents. My father's Uncle Billy lived there with us.

Number 84 was a typical 1890s terrace house erected to house miners and their families; my grandparents had moved there in 1902 and my father and his brother and sisters had been brought up there. It had a front parlour, reserved for Sunday use only, a middle room, a kitchen where nearly all household activity took place, and a pantry. Only the middle room and the kitchen had any form of lighting - a single gas mantle. No electricity. Upstairs there were four bedrooms. The lavatory was part of the house but its door was outside in the back yard where the "bosh", i.e. the earthenware sink under a cold water tap, was fixed to the house wall and open to the elements. Here we washed every day summer and winter as there was no water supply inside the house.

When war broke out the pits reopened and worked three shifts. We had a ton of free coal tipped onto the pavement near the hatch at the top of the garden, and the job of shovelling the coal through the hatch into the garden was one that Dewi and I often had to do, and it was a dusty and dirty pair who presented themselves for washing at the end of the day. In the evening Gran saw us to bed by carrying one of the several brass oil lamps which supplemented the gas mantles. The house was comfortable and warm, with coal fires in the middle room and the kitchen, burning continually in their black-leaded grates. In the kitchen the kettle seemed always on the boil, but one of the main tasks for the kitchen fire was to warm enough water for my uncle's bath when he came off shift at the colliery. Stripped to the waist bending over the tin tub in front of the fire he would wash his top half, with us children scrubbing his back, until we retired to the middle room whilst he washed his lower body in private.

The kitchen was also Uncle Billy's place. He was over 70 years old, my grandfather's brother and like his forebears been an ironworker - a chainmaker - rather than a collier. He bore the marks of his trade. One eye had been put out by a hot spark and he had lost two fingers of one hand. He used to sit in a Windsor armchair underneath the pendulum clock by the side of the fire, wearing a battered, greasy brown trilby hat and smoking his pipe. On Saturday nights he put on his best suit and paid sixpence to Dewi and me for putting on and lacing his boots, before going off to the "Llwyncelyn" to meet his friends.

Early days

At Christmas time Dewi and I walked to a bakery close to Birchgrove, sixpence clutched in one hand, carrying the cake which Gran and Aunt Sally had prepared for the baker's oven. Here it joined dozens of other cakes from surrounding families. We paid the baker his sixpence and the following day we collected our cake ready to be iced.

On a night before Christmas I remember Uncle Oliver staying up to tend the Christmas puddings cooking in a big pot over the middle room fire, removing puddings when they were done and replacing them with others. We ate reasonably well, but my lasting memory is relishing the *"bara te"* which Gran made, pieces of buttered bread placed in a bowl with hot, sweet tea poured over. We loved it!

Going to Pontypridd market with Gran was a regular event which always included a meal of faggots and peas eaten in a small room under a staircase in the Market Hall and served by an old lady dressed in a long black dress.

We attended the Band of Hope Sunday School at John Pugh Chapel in Porth, and enjoyed the annual chapel outings to Barry Island, by special train. Dewi went to Llwyncelyn school because he was two years older than me, whilst I went to St Mary Street junior school where my mother and Aunt Mary had been taught. At Llwyncelyn we often played with a iron hoop and stick made at the colliery blacksmith's by Oliver's butty, or we played "Cat and Dog" with two fashioned pieces of wood using one to hit the other and then to hit it again whilst in mid-air and send it spinning down the road, or we swung around the lamp post on a piece of rope.

Opposite Leslie Terrace was a very steep wooded bank beyond which were the railway and the river both spanned by the new road bridge to Trehafod, and the houses of Britannia. A long rope had been thrown over a high branch of an oak tree to be used as a spectacular swing out from the bank and over the track below.

We children spent very little of the daylight hours playing indoors; a lot of time was spent in exploring the hills (or mountains as we called them) and the nearby colliery reservoirs – Kemp's Pond and Coedcae.

The Forties
The streets were normally lit by gas but workmen removed the tops of the street gas lamps to comply with the wartime

blackout, and the Local Defence Volunteers (LDV) were formed, to parade in their suits in the football field at Nythbran with sticks instead of rifles. When Gran died in her sleep in January 1940, curtains were drawn and she was laid out in her coffin in the front parlour, as was the custom, with neighbours calling to pay their respects. Our parents travelled from London for the funeral. My father took me by the hand into the parlour to see her for the last time. When the cortege left the house the ladies and children stayed behind and only the men followed the hearse on foot, other men doffing their caps as it passed, as was the custom.

The "Blitz" began in September 1940 and in December our home in London was destroyed. For weeks my parents had to abandon Stepney each night and take to the deep shelters and, inevitably, one morning they returned to find that a bomb had destroyed the shop. The looters had got there first but they salvaged a few bits of furniture and headed back to Wales, staying in Llwyncelyn for a while, before buying a corner shop further up the Rhondda valley in Ton Pentre.

This was to be the first "home" with which I would properly identify and it is still important to me.

Ton Pentre

There had been an Iron Age settlement at Maindy but the village eventually grew around a farm until the deep mining of anthracite led in the nineteenth century to the development of terraced houses built to house the miners of Ton Pit, which overlooked the town from its position at the far end of one of its large spoil tips. Strangely, there was a bowling green at the end of the tip and a thriving club of which my father was once a member. However, the green was affected by subsidence and was a bit 'uneven'.

The shopping street was Church Road which had a bridge at each end; one led to Pentre and Ystrad, the other to Gelli and beyond. It had shops and a couple of pubs, the New Inn and the Windsor.

From Church Road other streets branched off and were crossed by other streets so, in its way, Ton was spread out and not strung out narrowly as were some of the valley towns.

Entertainment

There was a cinema at the Workmen's Hall and another, *The Grand*, in Pentre. The Ystradyfodwg Parish Church, St. Johns's, sat at the corner of Bailey Street and Church Road and there were a number of chapels. The Conservative Club in Queen Street, whose membership was entirely Labour, was popular and there were a few larger businesses such as the timber mill and the Hutchings' empire of butcher shop, slaughter house, electrical shop and garage. There was no rugby team but Ton Pentre Football Club had its home ground at the bottom of Parry Street, bordered by the river and the railway, alongside sidings for large coal trucks.

The "posh" part, where the terraced houses gave way to larger detached houses consisted of The Parade, Maindy Crescent and Maindy Croft. Generally, these were occupied by professional people such as teachers, doctors, and solicitors.

The Police Station and Magistrates Court were located at the bottom of the Parade directly opposite a back entrance to the yard of Ton Boys Junior School. Beyond Maindy Croft and perched on the hillside above the New Road which connected

Ton to Cwmparc and Treorchy was a small park; a children's playground with swings and roundabouts, two tennis courts and a small, little used novelty golf course.

The park-keeper's hut guarded the tennis courts and was manned by Archie, a tolerant, middle-aged man. Pentwyn Cottage Hospital was a half mile further up the New Road, supported from contributions by miners and public.

80 Bailey Street, was an end-of-terrace property built in the 1890's near the town end of the street. The houses were odd-numbered up one side and even-numbered back down the other so that numbers 1 and 80 faced each other, or nearly so. Lottie Bowen, teacher of pianoforte, lived in No.1 and had a brass plate to say so. (My mother begged me to learn the piano but I would not).

That side of the street had tiny front gardens enclosed by low walls, railings, and gates but on our side the front doors opened directly onto the pavement. Our shop was next to the Parish Church and its graveyard; immediately across the street was Bethesda Methodist Chapel, and both conducted their services in Welsh.

At the mid-point of the street Ton Boys Junior School stood alongside the brook which ran from the little valley above Ton Pit to the River Rhondda.

At the top end of Bailey Street were the stables for the Co-operative stores. Every morning a parade of horses drew their milk floats and bread carts along the street towards Church Road before fanning out to their different rounds; those few hundred yards from the stables to Bethesda chapel were enough to work the bowels of the horses so that the folk at our end of the street found a steady supply of garden fertiliser almost on their doorsteps.

Mr Tapper, (Fruit and Vegetables, Flowers and Funerals), lived at No.19 and had a shop in Church Road and Mr Hamer, coal merchant, lived in Brook House, the only detached house in Bailey Street.

Finally, opposite the Church were the offices of Crawshay Bailey Estate which owned considerable land and mineral rights: several streets were named after members of the families such as Bailey, Crawshay, Augusta, Clarence, Victoria....etc.

Bailey Street

Life in Ton
Regular visitors to the street were the Rag and Bone man, the Council Dust Lorry and the Pig Swill Cart from Maindy farm.

The dust (or ash) lorry called about twice a week to collect the refuse from each house; the name was appropriate because very little other than the ash from the coal fires was put out for collection and just one or two buckets was enough to contain it. Food packaging was not a problem!

The pig swill cart came to collect buckets of left over food, potato peelings, etc for Maindy farm, possibly as a war-time measure. The man (Old Tom) who led the horse and cart had a very weather-beaten face, wore highly polished leather gaiters and was bent double with rheumatism.

Then there were the Cockle Ladies dressed in long, old-fashioned clothes: they came by train from Swansea through the tunnel at Blaenrhondda to sell Lava Bread and cockles from wicker baskets - my father loved Lava Bread.

After the war, the *Shoni Onions* men came from France selling from bicycles festooned with strings of onions. A less welcome visitor was the flood which came to our part of Bailey Street whenever there was really heavy and continuous rain when the river rose well above its normal level. We were prepared for this by blocking the shop door with a large piece of wood backed by clay.

Transport

There wasn't much private traffic because of petrol rationing. Every hour the bus to Cardiff came from Treorchy and stopped outside the Co-op in Church Road. Other service buses ran along the almost continuous street of terraced houses that lined the valley from Porth to Blaenrhondda, passing through the separate, but seamlessly joined, towns on their way. Because pithead baths were yet to come, the workmen's buses on this road were filled with miners, clean on their way to work, blackened on their way home after the end of a shift signalled by the sounding of the colliery hooter, rather like a ship's horn.

Public transport dominated; one could walk along the middle of the road in relative safety. Alternatively, at Ystrad station there was a frequent train service from Blaenrhondda to Cardiff with connections at Porth and Pontypridd to numerous towns throughout South Wales. In those years there was a comprehensive railway network connecting all the valleys to each other and the outside world.

Health

Dr. Burke had a surgery just over Ton Bridge towards Gelli. We paid cash for treatment: money in hand, we sat in the waiting room with a crowd of other sufferers until called. I often went to get medicine for my father (I never knew what it was for) with a half-crown. It was Dr Burke who removed the warts from my hand at Pentwyn Hospital using a local anaesthetic and an electric knife when I was about eleven years old. I have not forgotten the sound and smell of my sizzling flesh, and he was concerned enough to offer me a glass of water when I said I was feeling dizzy. When boils arrived on my neck, as they do with teenagers, I went to Dr. John Jones who had a surgery in Cwmparc. He was just as sympathetic as Dr Burke.

The dentist in Pentre was more inclined to take teeth out rather than drill and fill, and maybe his patients preferred that, but there was treatment available through the school for us children. The surgery was in Treherbert and on the one occasion that I went there I had a tooth filled without local anaesthetic by an Irish lady who hummed and sang throughout the whole operation. I didn't.

The shop

I was 9 when we moved into the Bailey Street shop near Christmas 1940. Our new home had a side wall at an acute angle to the front, which resulted in odd-shaped rooms at that end of the house. My parent's bedroom was a small, windowless, triangular room which I was to use in later years as my darkroom when I took up photography, as did Roy Lewis and Dewi Griffiths. There was a shop area and an ice cream parlour at the front, and behind there was a living room and a small scullery.

My parents had the scullery re-built as a proper kitchen but we continued to live in just the one room after the work by Tom Davies, the builder, but there was water available inside the house, unlike at Llwyncelyn. Needless to say, entertaining was a bit limited by this lack of space - no question of taking home a girl friend to sit in the parlour!

There were four bedrooms, one of which was later converted into a bathroom and toilet. The garden was narrow and about ten to fifteen yards in length with the lavatory at the far end complete with candle and cut-up newspaper nailed to the door, and a coal shed to one side. A door opened from the garden onto the lane at the church side of the house, and this entry served not only our house but four other houses along Bailey Street; this was the way that coal was delivered to all five households. Mr Griffiths, who worked for the GWR railway company, lived next door at that time and on at least two occasions on a Sunday morning he took me with him when he did some checking up the line to Treherbert. This meant riding on the footplate of a railway engine which for a boy of my age was a great treat.

The shop sold all sorts of things in addition to the usual grocery items; bread, sweets, cigarettes, gas mantles, medicines, soaps, hair nets, combs, biscuits in glass-topped boxes, and ice cream. Until the war really hit home the ice cream parlour was in full swing and customers happily sampled our Knickerbocker Glories and Chocolate Sundaes. My job was to clean the ice cream making machine which involved a lot of scraping and licking to achieve perfect cleanliness - before all was properly cleaned in the kitchen! Unfortunately, the parlour did not survive for long; eventually it was used as a store for groceries and all the ice cream paraphernalia was packed away, never to be used again.

Generally, the shop opened each day at about 8.00 a.m. and closed at 6.00 p.m. with an hour for lunch; Thursday was half-day closing and it was not open on Sunday. We stayed open a bit later on Saturday to cater for the people queuing to get into second house at the Works cinema and who bought sweets and cigarettes for their night out. Quite a bit of shopping was conducted in Welsh since both my parents could speak the language and some of the older folk preferred it that way. The Rev. Alban Davies, minister for Bethesda, spoke nothing but Welsh to my parents in all the years that he shopped with them.

Social occasions

My father's birthday fell upon Christmas Eve and at the end of a very busy time in the shop. When the shop door was finally locked my mother poured herself a small sherry and started preparing Christmas dinner and my father put on his hat and headed for the back room of the Bridgend Hotel where his friends were already gathering. He was not a drinking man but he enjoyed a pint or two in the course of a week. When he came home he was often tipsy but never drunk, and he regularly brought a few friends with him (in the late 1940's it was often a small section of the Treorchy Male Voice Choir who favoured the Bridgend Hotel) and they would sing for my mother who would have been busy pouring tots of whisky for the visitors.

The back room of the Bridgend Hotel was almost like a club. After the war, when international rugby resumed, regular trips to matches in Scotland and Ireland would be organized and paid for by weekly contributions into a kitty. One occasional member was Dr. Burke, of whom it was said that he got on the train but never actually saw a game; he just enjoyed the company and the drinking.

The Cory Workman's Silver Band was another interest of my father. He served on the committee for a few years. I can't recall whether I volunteered or if it was expected of me, but for one season only on some Saturdays I found myself on the band's bus to the Cardiff City ground at Ninian Park where they performed before the kick-off and during half-time. My job, with other boys, was to shake collecting tins at the football fans as they poured through the turnstiles and, at half-time, to carry a tarpaulin around the playing pitch so that people could throw coins into it in appreciation of the band's playing. It didn't take us long to find out that the target was not the tarpaulin but the boys carrying it and we learned to be very wary and to duck quickly.

Six vertically challenged boys parading around the pitch!

My parents became friendly with Oswald (Dos) Jones and his

wife Beryl who lived nearby in Augusta Street. Their daughter, Pat, was two years younger than me but we became good friends in later years when she became a pupil at Pentre Sec. (Both Pat and I suspected that our parents thought that we would make a good couple). Sunday evenings would often be spent visiting each others homes and sharing a supper; then Pat and I would be expected to do our homework ready for the coming week. Other friends were Tom Daniels, manager of Hodge's outfitters in Llewellyn Street, his wife Betty and their daughter Nita.

Communications

We had no telephone, and television was then unheard of. If we needed to make a phone call then we walked 50 yards to the kiosk at the corner of Bailey Street. If it was a call to aunts in London, for instance, we had first to contact the operator and ask for "trunks" and then wait until the trunks operator answered and connected us. During the war a call to London could take up to 45 minutes of waiting before getting a connection for the three minute call. It was several years after the end of the war before a telephone was supplied to the shop. However, we did have a wireless, a brown bakelite model by GEC by which we got all the news and much entertainment from the BBC.

The newspapers of those years consisted of just one sheet of folded paper, that is, there were only four pages to carry all the news. My father favoured the *Daily Express* which we collected from the newsagent in Church Road and in the evening we read the *South Wales Echo* bought usually from an old man known as Johnny Echo who sold his papers tucked under his arm while parading the streets and shouting his wares.

Chapel

My mother was a Baptist and regularly attended Zion chapel in Pleasant View; my father, a Methodist, would visit Bethesda occasionally. Sometimes they went to chapel together, to Zion After trying the Baptist chapel I opted to go to the parish church next door to our house because many of my friends went there. After dressing in my Sunday Best I went to Sunday school (later, bible class), and evening service. I didn't make it to the choir with the other boys, but contented myself with pumping the organ when my turn came around and played a game to see how long I could delay pumping the organ before the music began to fade. Although I couldn't speak a word of Welsh I endured the services and could recite the proceedings by heart without understanding properly what I was saying!

Chores

Perhaps being the son of a grocer made my boyhood different from that of other boys.

My parents lived in their workplace and I shared it with them - and often worked with them by serving in the shop, delivering orders and fetching bread. I became a dab hand at cutting and packing groceries to conform with the ration rules; weighing so many ounces of sugar, butter, cheese, etc., all of which were delivered to the shop in bulk - sacks of sugar, great blocks of butter, and big cylinders of cheese (miners were entitled to a great deal of cheese!).

Opposite the shop lived David Morgan and his family. He was my father's accountant and friend. Once a year the annual stocktaking was done with his help; after the shop had closed on a Saturday we would work all evening and through the following Sunday counting, weighing and noting all the items in the shop: list after list until a final tally was reached to submit to the Inland Revenue.

Customers lodged their ration books with the shop which was then allocated the appropriate quantities of essential foodstuffs to be delivered by the wholesaler.

Cutting and serving the right weights to each customer was a problem because nobody wanted underweight butter, for example. My father used to complain that we seldom ate butter, using margarine instead, because there was none left for us once the customers had received their ration! In the same way we were customers of Hutchings' butcher shop where we queued for our weekly rations, consisting of a few ounces of meat and one egg per person per week. Both clothes and furniture were in short supply and could only be bought with coupons.

There were special occasions. Occasionally the wholesaler would deliver to our shop a box filled with luxuries; tins of peaches, pineapple, salmon etc which were then distributed to customers after checking a list which showed who had benefited on the last occasion. Everyone got a share in the end!

Allotments flourished with many families: Digging for Victory as the government urged meant fresh vegetables and fruit were plentiful. Bananas were different - these were not seen for years until, as was rumoured, a banana boat came into Cardiff. Once a week I helped to count the food ration coupons and delivered them the following day to the Food Office behind the Council Offices in Pentre. On busy days, when I was a bit older, I cooked meals whilst my parents served in the shop though it was generally something with a plate of chips.

Fetching the bread was something that my father usually did during the week, but my cousin Dewi and I would do it on Saturday (twice) and occasionally before going to school during the week. For this purpose my father had built a cart - a large, deep wooden box mounted on two pram wheels and covered with a piece of tarpaulin; inside there was a clean, white cotton sheet. Rain or shine we pushed this cart across Ton to Mr Jones' bakery in Gelli, in a small row of shops opposite the Pictoreum cinema. At the back door of the bakery the cart was filled with the daily variety of loaves - Swanseas, Cobs, Tins, Splits etc. The smell of fresh-baked bread was everywhere, and before pushing the cart back to the shop we would feast on the warm crusty bits that broke off the loaves as they were taken from the oven. Once Mr Jones had cleaned the bakery he changed into a smart suit: he was an insurance man collecting for the Pearl in Gelli and Ton, and he generally dropped by for a cup of tea and to settle the account with my father.

School

My cousin Dewi had come to live with us in Ton after Gran died: he went to Bronllwyn school, which he hated. We were both still speaking with cockney accents and I think that we must have stuck out like sore thumbs (although there were other evacuees in Ton), but our accents were gradually changing. By then I was going to Ton Boys Junior School which had just three or four classrooms each heated in winter by a large coal-fired stove surrounded by a protective iron guard; very tall windows admitted daylight. We sat in forms and were taught by Mr Morse and Mr Griffiths. The headmaster, Mr Williams, used a bamboo cane to impose discipline, and that practice put me into a particularly humiliating situation. Among the many items that my father had inherited when he bought the shop was a stock of canes, the sort for punishing small boys; thick canes, thin canes, whippy ones. Now and again, when the canes at the school were considered to be past their best, I was asked to run down the street to my father's shop and return with a new cane so that an unhappy boy could be properly beaten. My father didn't like it, and I certainly didn't, so he got rid of them.

I discovered during playtime that I was a quick runner, even in hob-nailed boots, and this led to my selection for the 100 yard sprint for the school at the Junior Sports Day at Gelligaled Park further down the valley.

I spent the best part of eighteen months in Ton Boys Junior

School before passing the 11 plus entrance examination in the summer of 1942 (93rd in the Rhondda! Phew!!) to attend Pentre Secondary Grammar School.

Many of the boys I met in Ton Boys School were to become long time acquaintances and friends even though, after passing the 11 plus examination, we went to different schools. John Evans, Malcolm (Nappy) Evans, John (Jackie) Hodder, Roger Williams, and John Winter did well enough to go to Porth County school. Elwyn Evans, Gwyn Evans, John Gale, Cedric Goodwin, and Keith Slade joined me in going to Pentre Sec. whilst Leighton Brunt went to Porth Sec. Dewi Griffiths, and a year behind him Roy Lewis, attended Pentre Sec and both became close friends. Dewi Griffiths' father had become the caretaker at the Workmen's Hall and the family lived in the accommodation at the back of the Hall - not a hundred yards from our shop. At that time Dewi's mother, Jinny, used to cut my hair in her living room, cigarette dangling between her lips. When I was older Bill Davies in Church Road was my barber

Games

We small boys played marbles in the gutter, games of chase in the school yard, caught sticklebacks in Ton brook, fished in the river Rhondda (black though it was with coal dust), and played on the Maindy, our local mountain. In the summer we camped on the side of the brook in the little valley beyond Ton pit, though were never so brave as to stay out for the night.

We sometimes stood at the doorway of Hutchings's abattoir to watch the men despatch sheep with a quick knife into the neck leaving them on their backs in a trough with their legs kicking the air - then the disembowelling. Well, it was something to view when there was not much else on offer.

In winter we slid down the Maindy slopes on home-made sledges and undertook expeditions in the snow to the Seven Lakes (small, peaty ponds in reality) on top of Maindy mountain. And, of course, we went to the pictures at the Works, i.e. the Workmen's Hall, when the price was just three-pence for a seat in the first two or three rows downstairs.

We had few toys (the only one I can recall was a model railway set which featured a clockwork Flying Scotsman running around a circular track pulling two carriages) since so much time was spent out of doors. We had bikes, a football, a cricket bat and, if the weather was bad, there were indoor games such as *Ludo, Snakes and Ladders*, and *Dominos*. Books and comics were read avidly: *The Dandy, Beano, Film Fun* when we younger, and *The Wizard* and *Hotspur* later on. The comics annuals received for Christmas were read and swapped. These pastimes didn't change much when I first went to Pentre Sec. but rugby, cycling and tennis were to become the main interests and so extend my circle of friends.

Grammar School

Pentre Secondary Grammar School - Pentre Sec. - was situated half way up the mountainside behind St. Peter's Church. A steep road wound its way uphill from Llewellyn Street and entered the gates below the two hard-surfaced tennis courts which served as playgrounds - one for boys, the other for girls. It was a three storey building built of stone edged by red brick; behind were two paved yards where the outside toilets were located, and beyond these yards the hillside rose steeply, scattered with trees.

The school took pupils from the upper part of the Rhondda Fawr while Tonypandy Sec looked after the middle section and Porth Sec. from the lower part. Ferndale Sec. drew its pupils from the Rhondda Fach and, distinct from these four schools, Porth County selected its pupils from both valleys, always those who had done best in the entrance examination.

Like all the boys, I was still wearing short trousers when I went to Pentre Sec. and usually we did not wear our first pair of longs until we entered our 'teens, some later than others.

There were about 400 pupils at the school spread through Forms 1 to Forms 5 and then on to first and second year sixth forms. Some children left school at the age of 14 or 15 years to start work but the rest stayed on to Form 5 and left after sitting the Central Welsh Board Examination (CWB). The certificate was awarded only if a credit had been achieved in five given subjects, otherwise you got nothing to record your secondary education.

On leaving, some went to work in local offices, shops, factories or coal mines and others to teacher training colleges. The sixth forms were very exclusive with about only a dozen or so pupils entering each year, split between an Arts or Science stream.

Because of the war there were a few young women on the staff and no young men. Miss Bebb was my first form teacher (Form 1a), teaching Latin and French throughout the school. She predicted I would not succeed at French because of my accent, and despaired of me in Latin because I would regularly gain negative marks in terminal exams, i.e. less than 0%. My second year was worse because the form teacher (Form 2b) was now Arthur Hanney, a bully and a brute who should never have been allowed into a school. He taught Geography and Maths with terrible consequences for his class and I just managed to avoid going down to Form 3c. My mathematics marks were truly dismal, so my parents paid for private tutoring in Maths after school hours.

Without Arthur Hanney things changed for much the better and I succeeded in passing CWB in eight subjects which would allow me to move into the sixth form where I took Physics, Maths and Chemistry. But not before I spent a second year in Form 5. Although I had passed all my subjects well, it was decided that I should have taken Chemistry for CWB and therefore must stay back to do so. There must have been great confusion, not least in my mind, because at the end of that second year I had still not taken the course in Chemistry! So, I studied the subject for both CWB and Higher School Certificate in my first year in the sixth form and passed the CWB quite well after just one year of study. I disliked Chemistry and looked forward to dropping the subject. In those final two years I also became a prefect and Head Boy for my last year.

It's difficult to recall who, in those last years, were in the fifth, first year sixth or second year sixth forms. It did not seem to matter as long as there was some other activity which brought you together, and in most cases it was sport or examinations. There was Berwyn Thomas, Islwyn Thomas, Ron

Kinsey, Dewi Griffiths, Roy Lewis, Gwyn Evans and Des Francis. The girls included Pat Leyland from Ton, Jean Cleaver from Gelli, Enid Benbow and Marilyn Davies from Treorchy, all good athletes as well being very attractive! There was also the enigmatic Mary Pugh from Pentre, Pat Jones from Ton and Eileen Bennett from Treherbert, all girls I recall quite well.

Berwyn became a consultant anaesthetist in Cardiff, and Islwyn went into teaching. Ron lived in Treorchy with his grandmother and uncle, his parents having disappeared. Their house had little furniture and on one occasion, when I visited, his grandmother was wringing the neck of a chicken in the middle room!

Ron was intelligent but had little support or guidance. After passing Higher he drifted into all sorts of jobs becoming a spider-man erecting steelwork on high rise buildings, and (if I believed him) diving for pearls in the Pacific.

Dewi was a born entertainer, an extrovert. He perfected an act in which he mimed the songs and action of the film actor, Danny Kaye, which he performed in and out of school. He was billed in the music halls as "*The Welsh Danny Kaye*". He later forged a successful career with the BBC.

Roy was a bit intense, thoughtful, with a dry sense of humour He was in the Arts stream, and later he studied law, was called to the bar and then followed a successful career in Education becoming first One of Her Majesty's Inspector of Schools and then a College Principal and a successful author of crime fiction.

Gwyn left school and joined the Rhondda Council finally to

become the Chief Executive of the Rhondda Borough Council. He had a lovely singing voice at school and never the lost the gift.

Des Francis came to the school in Form 3 when his policeman father was promoted to sergeant and posted to Ton Pentre. A sporting family, they lived at the top end of Bailey Street and it was natural for me to meet Des on the way to school. Rugby and cricket were their loves and Des' Uncle Jack seldom missed watching the school XV playing at the Oval in Treorchy. I used to go to Cardiff Arms Park with Des to watch Glamorgan play cricket. Des and his family moved back to the Swansea area at about the time we were entering the sixth form. Eventually, he went to work in a bank.

Donald Davies and Mike Welsh were one year ahead of me and took Science subjects, later making careers in those disciplines, Donald in Education and Mike in Industry (Bridgwater). I came to know Donald better after I left Pentre Sec but Mike and I got together whilst in school to cycle to Land's End using the YHA hostels.

The one thing all these boys had in common was a great sense of humour; not a miserable face amongst the lot!

School staff

Mr Hugh, the headmaster, joined the school in the same year as me. He was a popular headmaster. I was caned by him twice in my progress through school: my parents never knew. An elderly Miss Harris was the Deputy Head, taught History and was famous for her exhortation to any girls passing through the Assembly Hall (aka the gym) when boys would be using it for

P.E. to do so 'looking neither to the left nor to the right'. Miss Bebb, my first form mistress and teacher of French and Latin, was a spinster who had a Gentleman Friend, who lived on our side of Bailey Street. They walked out together regularly for years and it was said that she would not marry until her aged and ailing father no longer needed her care. I hope that they did marry, eventually.

The teachers with whom I was significantly involved in those later years at Pentre were the elderly and benign Physics master Mr James (Jimmy Fizz), Abbie Davies the Chemistry master, and Tudor Davies our Maths master: he belonged to the Royal College of Organists, was an accomplished pianist, the conductor of a Male Voice Choir in Treorchy, and a keen cricketer. Occasionally, on rainy days at lunchtime, when we could not play outside, he would give an impromptu piano recital in the Assembly Hall. On a summer day, when he was satisfied with our maths progress in the sixth form, he would take us out to the tennis courts to enjoy a little cricket practice instead of repeating some aspect of mathematics. We thought a lot of Tudor!

When the war ended younger men joined the staff; Idwal Morgan to teach English alongside the established Potty (Mr Lewis), and Eddie Thomas joined Jimmy Fizz to teach Physics. Although in Bill Davies we had a teacher who taught P.E., Sport and Craftwork, it was Eddie Thomas and Tudor Davies who looked after the rugby and cricket teams, respectively.

Each school day began with Assembly when the entire school gathered in the Hall to say prayers, sing a couple of hymns and listen to the day's announcements. Very occasionally we were told of the death of a former pupil in the war.

School Eisteddfods

March 1st, St David's Day, was a significant day for the school. The occasion was celebrated in style with competitions between the four Houses into which the school was divided, each with its own Captain - *Carfan, Illtyd, Mabon and Tathan*. Preparations started straight after the Xmas holidays with pupils entering competitions in essay writing, poetry, languages, art, woodwork, and music. Choral practice at lunch time started immediately. The whole came together during a two day concert in the assembly hall when musicians, singers and choirs performed before the whole school and the judges.

On the last day the headmaster would announce the name of the winning House, and the Captain of that House would be ceremoniously chaired (in the school's bardic chair) surrounded by the prefects all dressed in bardic robes. A sword was produced; the headmaster, also dressed in bardic robes, held it above the head of the seated Captain and drew it from its scabbard. "*A oes heddwch?*" (Is there Peace?) he would ask. "*Heddwch*" would come the loud response from the assembled school at which the sword was thrust back into its scabbard. This was done three times before the House Captain was paraded out of the hall to loud cheers. Photographs were taken by Norman Studios and the rest of the week was declared a school holiday. My House was *Tathan*; it always came last with *Mabon* always the winner, it seemed. This was odd since the membership of the Houses was by random selection.

My contributions were entries in technical drawing, and woodwork, (I was pretty good at both gaining a Distinction in CWB, the first Mr 'Blocky' Evans our Woodwork teacher had seen in years), Only on one occasion did I sing in the *Parti Wyth* singing competition (Party of Eight - two sopranos, two contraltos, two tenors, and two baritones). Membership of the House Choir was compulsory!

Sport

There were teams for Rugby, Hockey (for the girls), Cricket, and Athletics: although we had tennis courts nobody actually played the game. Because of its situation on a steep hillside there were no sports facilities at the school so rugby games were played at The Oval, Treorchy with dressing rooms at Treorchy Boys Club, as was any training for Athletics. The school population was too small to be able to run more than one team at each sport so there were no Junior teams or Second XV for rugby, and no competitive games seemed to begin until the third or fourth form when you might be chosen to play for one of the school teams.

I played rugby for the school until I left for college, first at wing three-quarter but later as a centre three-quarter and, in my last year, I was made captain of the rugby team. I had already taken my turn as secretary for the team which meant compiling the fixture list, engaging and paying a referee for home games - usually Rhys Morgan Rees from Treorchy (his fee was 2/6d), booking the changing room at *The Red Lion* pub in Treorchy High Street - and hiring buses for away fixtures.

There were other rugby teams and other matches. I played for

Treorchy Boys Club for a while, and ad hoc teams that were assembled from time to time. The most memorable games were against Porth County whether at school level or at former pupils level. There was quite a bit of rivalry between the two schools. The Old Boys matches took place after the war and might have been memorial games. They gathered together some quite famous names in Welsh rugby; Billy Cleaver from Pentre and Cliff Jones from Porth, two famous outside halves, Gordon Wells, another Welsh cap, and a number of county and club players. For each game one boy from each school was invited either to play or run the line and I was chosen to be a linesman one year, when I shared a dressing room with Cliff Jones who was then the referee, and the following year I played on the wing when Billy Cleaver played at outside half.

Eddie Thomas featured in these games. He was both a former pupil and, at that time, a Physics master at Pentre so he qualified twice over. He had come to the school immediately after the war and straightway took care of the rugby team; at first he played for Treorchy RFC, then Neath but he finally settled with Cardiff RFC and later became their captain.

I ran the 100 yard and 220 yard sprints and medley relays and became captain of the athletics team in my last year. I was not a bad sprinter but a bit diffident; athletics training was not a big issue despite the fact that we had at school a Welsh Schools champion sprinter in Roy Wynne, who had been captain before me and had been selected to play for Welsh Secondary Schools XV on the wing. So, for most of the time I ran in the shadow of Roy though there were very rare times when I would get the better of him - probably on one of his off days! Occasionally we would collect a small team together and compete in the Miner's Day Sports at Pontypridd with the hope of winning a voucher for sports goods; no cash prizes then as everything was strictly amateur.

I was not a cricketer. Roy Lewis and Des Francis were keen players. I played in a proper game only once when the school team were a man short for a game at Tonyrefail. They dressed me in whites, put me in as last man to bat and I was out second ball from a fast bowler. But honour had been satisfied - the school had turned up with a full team. Everyone was happy!

There was a School Club at which end-of-term dances were held and pupils from other schools would be invited to evening meetings when there would be dancing and debates and, in return, we would be invited to their functions. The meetings were not very regular - but it was where most boys learned to dance with the help of the girls. Thus, when I was in the sixth form, I met my first proper girl friend - a girl from Porth Sec. Later in our friendship, when I was introduced to her family in Porth, her mother said "Oh, so you're Morfydd's boy!" which placed me immediately as being "of Porth" - our mothers had gone to school together!

Between playing rugby and going to School Club parties I was introduced to the pleasure of a pint of beer. Sometimes we boys had to use the dressing rooms at the *Red Lion* pub where Treorchy RFC was based, and it was usual then to have a drink (just one) after the game whilst waiting your turn to get into the hot bath. Quite illegal!

The same thing happened when we played in Ogmore but it was not the norm; drinking was not something we regularly indulged in. Eddie Thomas was the tempter at party time when he would take a few of the rugby-playing sixth-formers down to a pub in Pentre for a quick drink before the party. Then, carefully chewing chlorophyll sweets to remove the smell of beer from our breath, we weaved our way up the hill to the school!

The school magazine was titled "*The Axe*" derived from the school motto "*Hog dy Fwyall*", which in English was "Whet thy axe". It was produced by the sixth forms twice a year and cyclostyled in the stockroom. The headmaster's secretary typed all the material onto skins which were then attached to the printer, after which it was a case of turning a handle to print the pages. It was always a problem to get enough material and articles were written by both staff and pupils, but there was a gossip column (Dewi's job) and the fortunes of the various sports teams were included. This was the vehicle by which Roy Lewis published his first short stories; the start of a prolific writing career.

Holidays

Because of the shop my parents were never able to go on a long holiday and, obviously, I never went on a family holiday. Once or twice, when I was younger, my bike and I were put on the train to Bridgwater where I would spend the summer holidays with my mother's sister, Aunt Mary, and my cousins Thelma, Ruth and Gordon, all older than me but great fun. I enjoyed those days in Somerset, cycling around the country lanes.

Otherwise I would spend my time with friends in Ton Pentre doing things that boys normally do!

I had a new bike when I was about 13 years old. An orange-painted Raleigh all-steel bicycle with dropped handle bars and a 3-Speed Sturmey Archer gear, and on this I explored most of the Vale of Glamorgan, usually by myself.

Because of the war all signposts had been removed from crossroads and junctions, and without a map you could easily get lost. And maps could not be bought. So, I would copy sections from an old and tattered map and use them for navigating the lanes of the Vale where once or twice I came across working parties of Italian prisoners of war doing farm work.

At 15 years of age I joined the Youth Hostels Association and made my first visit to a hostel. I pedalled over the Rhigos mountain to reach the Storey Arms hostel at the foot of the Brecon Beacons and, after a miserably cold night in a bunk bed with thin blankets, climbed to the top of Pen y Fan and Corn Ddu before cycling back home.

I was enthusiastic about the YHA; it became an important feature of summer holidays for some years after this as I cycle-toured with my friends; to north Wales and Snowdon; across the south of England to Canterbury; and twice to Land's End. Four tours all told. But there were frequent rides to the seaside at Porthcawl and Barry via the Bwlch mountain and down the Ogmore valley to Bridgend and beyond, and at other times over the Rhigos mountain to Pont-Nedd-Fechan to explore the caves and waterfalls.

Social matters

What else did we do with our time out of school? There was rugby, tennis, and social matters such as going to birthday parties; meeting for coffee in the Bracchi shops (cafés owned by Italian families) promenading on the New Road on summer Sundays; these things occupied us in our 'teens, and in all this I was associated with two groups of friends whose activities overlapped.

First was the Ton group, which included John Evans, John Winter, Malcolm Evans (Nappy), Roger Williams, John Jenkins and Peter Philips all of whom lived quite close to me. In the evenings we might meet in the Lounge at Rabiotti's *Bridgend Café*, to chat. All these boys had been to Ton Boys School but apart from me they all attended Porth County.

John Evans' father was the Principal of the Treforest School of Mines, and the family lived in Maindy Croft. I'd call for John early on a summer morning and we'd climb over the fence of the nearby park to play tennis until the park-keeper, Archie, arrived to make us all a cup of tea and collect a little cash for the council fee.

John Winter lived in Parry Street, son of a miner, and Nappy in Llanfoist Street. Nappy was a happy-go-lucky lad who later studied engineering at Treforest and married Barbara in Tonypandy, memorable for the reception and the hymns that Nappy chose for the ceremony. He died in a car crash in the Channel Islands whilst still in his thirties. Roger Williams was the keen tennis player from Clara Street (even in those early years he used to go up to London to watch the Wimbledon

Championships) and after school he joined H.M. Customs and Excise in Swansea.

John Jenkins, from Upper Canning Street, was a year or two younger than me, a sprinter who played rugby on the wing for Porth County Sadly, he died as a young married man. Peter Philips was the son of the manager of Ton Pit and lived in a detached house close to the pit - *Brynmafonydd* - not far from Maindy Farm. Peter and I helped with hay-making when I was either in Ton Boys or the first year or so in Pentre Sec. Later, when I was older, I became aware of the fact that he had two very attractive cousins in Mair and Enid Philips of Cwmparc, both of whom went to Pentre Sec. Peter was a good middle-distance runner, became a RAF fighter pilot and was killed in an air accident in his mid-twenties.

I spent more time with the other group which included Roy Lewis, Brian Roberts, Dewi Griffiths, Gwyn Evans, Leighton Brunt, Keith Lewis, Mansel Lloyd, and Jackie Hodder. We indulged in theatrical/broadcasting schemes in the attics of the Workmen's Hall with Dewi, played rugby, promenaded to Treorchy and spent evenings there in Dom's café drinking milk shakes. Brian Roberts lived in Lloyd Street, Gelli, close to Keith Noakes who joined us on a YHA tour one year - and only one year! Somehow he got up our noses: we were secretly increasing the height of his saddle by a little bit each day in the hope that he would get a sore backside.

Brian was a Porth County boy who was blind in one eye as a result of an airgun pellet so was forbidden to play rugby with the rest of us. Leighton lived in Wyndham Street below Roy and Keith in Kennard Street: he was with me at Ton Boys School but had gone to Porth Sec after the 11+ examination. A good rugby player, he played for his school team just as Roy and I did for Pentre Sec. and Keith for Porth County. It was common for us all to spend hours kicking the ball about on the pitch on the tip behind Roy's house in Kennard Street or in the yard of Ton Boys School.

On the Waun with Dewi, Roy and Prince

Boys from the two groups often joined forces to go on those YHA cycling tours in the summer holidays, and to make up ad hoc rugby teams to play against equally occasional teams. On Saturdays, after playing for the school in the morning, we often caught a train to Cardiff and went straight to the Arms Park to watch Cardiff RFC play. Memories of Jack Matthews, Bleddyn Williams, Billy Cleaver and Haydn Tanner!

Sunday promenading up and down the New Road was a normal social practice and it wasn't confined to youngsters. It seemed that everybody did it after chapel on a Sunday evening. It was the way in which people met and exchanged news, and it was also the way that boy met girl with a lot of nudging, laughing and giggling from their friends! Occasionally, chapel ministers (such as Rev. Alban Davies) got on their soap boxes on the patch of grass opposite Pentwyn hospital to preach to the crowds.

Friday evening was usually reserved for a visit to the Library in the old school in Pleasant View in Pentre. Here we would stock up with books for the coming week before retiring, when we were older, to the Bridgend café for coffee and talk. At first I read the *William* books by Richmal Compton and Capt.W.E. Johns's *Biggles* adventures, then later on Dornford Yates, Dennis Wheatley, Rafael Sabatini, Victor Hugo, Zane Gray, and the Westerns of Oliver Strange. Reading was a major pastime.

The War Years

From the time that I was evacuated from London and the destruction of our home in Stepney, to moving to Ton Pentre, and the years that followed, our lives were influenced by the war. My cousin Dewi went back to London before the war ended and before the D-Day landings in France when he was 14 and I was 12 years old. We had been together, almost as brothers, for nearly five years. There were still dangers in London from both V1 and V2 rocket raids but nevertheless he went back to school in Bow and later became an apprenticed electrician.

Apart from the rationing of food and other commodities there were many other reminders that things were not peaceful. My cousin Arthur was killed piloting a Lancaster bomber on a raid over Germany; his plane crashed in Denmark where he is buried together with his crew. His mother, Aunt Margaret, had been an occasional visitor but she came more often because a new neighbour professed to be a spiritualist and Aunt Margaret found some solace in visiting her.

My father was turned down for military service despite his years in the army and so he took up A.R.P. duties. I recall the blackout restrictions; the Home Guard manoeuvres that took place in the streets, and machine gun practice in the valley beyond Ton Pit; and there was the bombing of Cwmparc and Ystrad in April 1941 when my father went on duty and we sheltered under the table .

One day I was with pals on Pentre mountain when a Spitfire flew overhead, crashed into Maindy mountain and the pilot was killed. We raced down the mountain, across Ton and made for the crash site but were stopped on the way. It was rumoured that Mr Morgan, the farmer, had "killed" his horse in an effort to get to the crash site!

And then there was the arrival of the Americans, the GI's, in Pentre in early 1944. The men were barracked in the old Pentre Hotel and the officers in people's homes. Children begged their parents to host an officer, me included, but there was no room in our house. The GI's were generous with sweets and nylon stockings - and a great attraction for the young women; the children greeted the soldiers with "Got any gum chum?" in the hope of a hand-out. In early June we got up one morning to find that they had all disappeared quietly overnight; the invasion of Europe was under way.

I left Ton Pentre in September 1950 to go to Swansea

University College. My parents had bought me my first dressing gown at Hodges and a trunk at E.H.Davies in Pentre and when this was packed it was put on the train to Swansea which then went up the valley to Blaenrhondda, through the tunnel, and down the Afan valley to Neath and beyond.

Thereafter, I came home only for occasional week-ends and holidays, some of them shortened when I would find a temporary holiday job away from the valley. After graduation my first job was in the Midlands and the visits were less frequent.

In truth, like many others, without knowing it at the time I had left the Rhondda for good.

Dewi, Roy, Ken & Brian 1949

Later Years

After leaving Swansea University College I took my first job and joined Armstrong Whitworth Aircraft Co. in Coventry in the Guided Weapons Division. The company was engaged in developing a Ship-to-Air missile for the Royal Navy. The post fell into the category of a reserved occupation so it meant I was excused National Service. I also had to sign the Official Secrets Act so when my friends asked me what I was doing I had to be somewhat reticent and provide no details: maybe they thought I was a spy!

I spent two years in Coventry before I obtained a transfer to The Royal Aircraft Establishment at Aberporth, in Cardiganshire. There I was given more responsibility being Deputy in charge of the AWA facility. I was also supervising the staff responsible for liaison with the RAE and the Royal Navy who were then involved in launching test missiles and the consequent retrieval of data thereafter.

In 1958 there came a change of direction in my career. I left AWA to start work in the commercial field, being employed by the Atomic Power Division of English Electric in Leicester. I was now working for a company which was part of a consortium of companies, engaged in the construction of one of the first commercial nuclear power stations at Hinckley Point in Somerset. My new post meant I was working in the Applied Physics section: this principally involved testing materials for reactor shielding and preparing instrumentation for eventual reactor commissioning. I was later promoted to become Section Leader.

This was a time when the civil reactor programme was expanding and the Central Electricity Generating Board was growing considerably, as the various power stations were being built. I visited the north east regularly, when the power station at Hartlepool was being built. I usually stayed in Darlington but took the opportunity to wander around the area, visiting Seaton Carew (where it seems Roy Lewis now lives). The CEGB was responsible for their safe and efficient operation of these stations, and I served on a committee which overlooked the commissioning of new operations. It was in the process also of establishing the Berkeley Nuclear Laboratories. These were located in Gloucestershire and the CEGB was meanwhile recruiting staff in many disciplines to work there.

I applied to join them and was appointed to BNL in 1961 to work in the Applied Physics Division. Initially I was engaged in fuel safety studies in the early Magnox reactors. Later I was called upon to continue the work on the Advanced Gas-Cooled Reactors. I continued working in Gloucestershire for the rest of my career, ending up as a Section Leader involved in the fuel commissioning of the AGR power stations. After that, retirement beckoned.

When I was working in Leicester I had met and married Catherine Ratnett, and when we moved to Gloucestershire our two children, Helen and David, were born and brought up there. They never moved away from their roots in a small market town in the south of the county. Kate's great interest was music and the piano but she also shared my love of walking and cycling – these were my main leisure pursuits, along with mountaineering, and fell-walking in Cumbria (where I had occasion to renew my acquaintance with Roy Lewis, who was then living in a 17th century farmhouse near Kirkby Stephen)

In retirement

GWYNFRYN EVANS

THE EVANS CLAN was a prolific one. The linked families tended to be large. My own paternal grandparents produced six children of whom only three survived. Other branches had similarly large families so that from an early age I was aware that I had a wide range of cousins .One of them, Uncle Meirion's son Buck (he gloried in the name John Graham Buckley Evans) was brought up in Cwmparc and was the only one who was enrolled at Pentre Grammar School at about the same time as me. He eventually became a primary school head teacher and was reckoned at school to be a fair rugby player. He married a local girl who had moved to Bailey Street in Ton after being bombed out of her home in in Cwmparc.. She was called Mary Morris and after they married they settled back in Cwmparc.

My father, Clifford was the son of John and Sarah Evans: he had three brothers and three sisters: cousin Buck was the son of Aunt Morfydd. As a young man, Clifford obtained work in the local colliery and married Haulwen Evans. And his leisure pursuit, alongside his brother John Morgan was outdoor bowls at Gelli Park.

The girl I married, Beti Davies also came from a large family: she was one of seven children, four of whom became teachers.

The Thirties

I was born at 62 Rees Street Gelli in August 1931: but my parents did not follow family tradition in respect of large families::my only brother Mal was not to arrive until 1937. We were both baptised in Hebron Chapel in Ton which the family regularly attended. In those days there was a congregation of over 200. When I was young my grandfather Lewis always took me to chapel every Sunday morning and Sunday School in the afternoon. I had to learn two psalms off by heart and I performed in the pulpit. I feel that I benefitted from this in later life and I've never been worried about speaking in public.

Hebron Chapel often staged musical shows and I was called upon to take the lead in two of these: I took the lead in two operettas: *Jack Frost* and *The Idea*. Performing in public at such a young age was good training for the future, and it gave me confidence that I had lacked as a youngster in the Infants School and Ton Boys School.

It was in Hebron that I met Beti. She had attended Porth Sec as did Leighton Brunt. Beti and I were married in 1954: we little guessed at that time that we would one day be celebrating our Diamond Wedding Party. That was a wonderful experience with many old friends turning up to celebrate with us.

I have served for years as a deacon in Hebron Chapel, and as its Secretary and Treasurer. My brother Mal also served as deacon. Sadly, the congregation is not what it used to be: now it consists of only about 12 members.

When my parents married they set up home in 62 Rees Street, Gelli along with my spinster aunt Gweneira (a strong Pentecostal) ; my grandparents Lewis and Mary Ann Evans also lived with us. Multiple occupation in Rhondda terrace houses was common enough in those days: some houses would have as many as three families in occupation, amounting to perhaps 11 people, grandparents, parents and children, and the men, who would be employed in the pits, would be forced to work alternate shifts—"hotbedding" in turn in the three or four-bedroomed houses. Also, the lack of inside bathrooms and no pithead baths, meant that everyone used tin baths and washed in the kitchen. We suffered from cockroaches, of course: most people did. We caught them by placing a bowl filled with bread on the floor overnight: the bowl teemed with them in the morning.

My grandmother Mary Ann was the daughter of a butcher in Pentre, called John Thomas. After Mary Ann's mother died her father married again and the 19 year old Mary Ann swiftly married Lewis Evans. She confided in me years later that she had married at such a young age mainly to get away from her stepmother. Lewis and Mary Ann produced 6 children of whom only 3 survived.

The township of Gelli was located the other side of the Incline from Ton Pentre: the incline held a single track railway down which loaded coal tubs were winched by steel cable to the sidings on the valley floor, beside the football field. The tubs were unloaded there into large trucks which conveyed the coal to Cardiff Docks. The empty tubs were then hauled back up to Bwyllfa Colliery and were a target for adventurous young boys seeking a ride, albeit brief, back up the incline.

Gelli boasted a few shops and a pharmacy in Gelli Road but shopping was mostly done in Church Street, Ton Pentre where there was a Co-operative Store, two barbers, three "*bracchi*" shops and several pubs as well as the ubiquitous chapels. The so called bracchi shops were cafés selling coffee, sweets and ice-cream: the shop owner might advertise himself as Forgione or Rabaiotti or some other Italian name but the shops were commonly referred to as bracchis. This was because such cafés had originally been established by the Bracchi family who had arrived in the valleys in the 1890s and established a chain of such establishments in the Rhondda and elsewhere in Wales.

Overlooking Gelli was a still active pit, the Gelli Colliery with its menacing slag heap. The pit provided employment for the local mining community but my father himself worked two miles up the valley in Cwmparc where there were two collieries, the Parc and the Dare. Like many other pitmen over the years he contracted "dust"—the stone-like sediment which prevented the lungs expanding. It was this pneumoconiosis which led to his retirement in 1957. By that time he had been promoted to the position of fireman in the pit.

But he survived until he was 80; my beloved mother passed away at the age of 87.

My early memories of the thirties include visits to mid-Wales to my aunt Maglone's home in Dinas Mawddwy. We visited them regularly when I was a child. On such occasions I vividly remember my grandfather John taking me up on the mountain and introducing me to the old country skills of fishing by hand for salmon in local streams, and rabbit snaring in the fields. Back in Gelli the stony, dirty lane behind the houses had not been made up and its surface was rough but it provided a location for us to play football with tennis balls. The greater part of our carefree young leisure time was spent on the Eastern tip, however: its dirty shale surface had been flattened by unemployed miners during the Depression as a way of passing their time and keeping fit during those gloomy, bitter days. A football pitch had been marked out and: goal posts had been erected so organised games between streets could be played and there was even a patch of grass where games of tennis and cricket could be played.

Over the years the area decayed, of course, the grass becoming scruffy and worn, the goalposts leaning crazily until they fell down. But it served as a great playground in its day: the tip was also a fine place for sledging in winter, usually on improvised pieces of discarded tinplate. If we wandered too close to the still working Bwllfa Pit however we were chased off by the formidable—and terrifying—Mr Eagel, in charge of keeping us kids out of mischief at the mine.

Always available as a playground was the mountain: behind Kennard Street was a decaying golf course (opened by the Duke of York and behind that the towering face of the mountain we knew as *The Seven Giants*, from the rock faces it presented.

And we got into mischief, of course, as boys do: there was a game we called *Fingers*: it involved tying tins to brass door knockers, knocking the door then running away to hide from the clattering that was caused when the door was opened.

One bonfire night we put a firework through the door of Mr Hughes the draper in Gelli: he lived in a big house near Bwllfa Cottages. It burnt a coat hanging behind the door. We were lucky to get away with it, not getting caught--Colin Hodson (known as Archie) was the son of the local Bobby. He was one of the gang!

I was able to apply the country skills learned from my grandfather by fishing for sticklebacks in the brook beside Ton Boys School with school friends Keith Slade and Mansel Coleman. We kept the plundered fish in glass jars until they sickened: they would get disposed of down the toilet. I put my mid-Wales acquired trout fishing skills to good account in the Rhondda river by Gelli Park.

The water was black with coal dust discharged from the collieries—except when the pits closed for Easter holidays—but the fish didn't seem to mind either way. I used a home-made bamboo implement as a rod and much envied the proper rods used by Keith and Mansel. I also envied the fact they caught more fish than I ever did!

I started at Ton Infants school in 1934—and hated it. The headmistress, Mrs Evans was the daughter of local undertaker Ivor Jones. At that age I lacked confidence and I regularly ran home to Rees Street during playtime. My mother was forced to take me back.

I was not alone in my early distress: I remember John Hodder, who was in my class, wetting his pants in terror in the playground and crying for his mother. Perhaps our early joint experiences welded the friendship that we have enjoyed ever since. John was clever at school once he settled down: he later went to Porth County and joined the Rhondda Council as a clerk. John was never particularly ambitious but he ended up as Chief Registration Officer. Elections always worked smoothly under his supervision. He was brilliant at his job and everything went like clockwork.

St Davids Street—and Dolwen-- snowbound

I was his boss for 20 years: he still lives in Pentre and we are very good friends. When the time came to leave the Infants School it was a proud day for us all: after three years in the

Infants we were going to the "big school"! I remember vividly how we gathered to join the crocodile group trailing up to Ton Junior Boys that autumn day in 1937:-I was a very proud marcher alongside companions Dewi Griffiths, Derek Jones, Keith Slade, Leighton Brunt and others. We were all excited, though some girls were clearly fearful, weeping nervously en route to the girls' school.

Settling in at Ton Boys School was difficult: I still lacked confidence and I hated Monday mornings when we had to learn our tables from a clock on the wall. If we made any errors we were rewarded by a stroke of a bamboo cane on our hands. I often grabbed the iron support under my desk on such occasions to ease the pain of my smarting hand. A wonderful way to teach young children!

The situation became so bad in that first year, I was so scared at returning to school for fear of further canings that my grandfather. Lewis Evans and my father coming straight from work took me to see Tom Rees, the headmaster. He was very sympathetic and understanding: he related to me the story of a young boy climbing a glass mountain. The boy failed to reach the top on several occasions but kept on trying until he succeeded. This worked for me, I got the message and from that moment onwards I improved quickly.

The main objective of the five years spent at Ton Boys School was to prepare for the examinations taken at 11 years, which would allow entry to secondary education—for those who passed! But the system was a flawed one: it was the teachers who decided who was likely to pass, and in fact the majority of the class were not allowed to enter the examinations.. Dewi Griffiths was one of these prevented from sitting and accordingly entered Bronllwyn Secondary Modern School. But there was also a certain flexibility: at the end of the first year those deemed not to be profiting from a grammar school education were transferred to Bronllwyn: those who did well at the Secondary Modern School were transferred to the grammar school.

Dewi was one of the latter; Mansel Lloyd, on the other hand started in Pentre Grammar but was then transferred to Bodringallt Technical School. In view of the later successful careers enjoyed by these two, and many others, one cannot say much for the judgment of primary school teachers in the late thirties!

I was lucky enough to be one of the few in my year selected to enter the 11+ examinations. The main tests were English and Arithmetic. When the results were printed in due course in the *Rhondda Leader* I discovered I had been placed at 137th in the Rhondda. It meant selection for a grammar school, but not for the first in the pecking order, Porth County. I was offered a place at Pentre Grammar..

The Forties

.When the Second World War began things were quiet enough to begin with—the false peace. But it was not long before Cardiff Docks became a target for German bombs. Accordingly, there were regular warning sirens to take cover. Like others in Ton Pentre we had no Anderson shelter outside in the yard so my brother Mal and I slept under the stairs when the local colliery hooter and siren went.

I remember the local library being destroyed by a bomb: the librarian was killed. On the same night bombs were dropped on the mountain overlooking my street, possibly intended to bring about the destruction of Gelli Colliery.

Cwmparc also suffered a night attack during which some 20 residents were killed. I remember the large attendance at the funeral. My father that awful night walked home from the colliery in his stockinged feet, admitting to the family that he was feeling very frightened .The German warplanes could have been seeking to knock out the Parc and Dare pits in Cwmparc but the more generally held theory was that the planes had probably failed to target their main objectives in Cardiff and had simply unloaded themselves of remaining bombs when returning to their bases.

It was in 1941 that I first fell in love –at the age of 10. Evacuees had arrived in the Rhondda in 1940, many from Cardiff and some from London. I first met Pauline Jenkins in Gelli Park: she had been evacuated to Rees Street in Gelli with her sister Sylvia, while her two brothers were placed in Lloyd Street. Pauline and I shared a kiss on the seesaw in the park playground but she soon returned to London. I still remember the date: 5th September 1941. Her address was 47 Greatdown Road, Harrow W7. Her return home devastated me at the time: I never heard from her again, but I still remember her fondly.

School Days

The Rhondda was unlike other areas in terms of the supply of grammar schools. Education was highly prized by most families—it was a way for a boy to escape the hot, dirty darkness of the dangerous work underground. And there was a preponderance of grammar schools. Accordingly, some 64% of the 11 year olds in Rhondda went to grammar schools: by contrast, at the same time in Essex the figure was about 24%. My position in the table meant I missed selection for Porth County: they took the "cream". I was allocated a place at Pentre Secondary Grammar School (known as Pentre Sec). In September 1942 I found myself placed in Form 1C but after examinations at the end of term I moved up to IB, and then in the second year, 2A.

I was good in Maths and languages and from the choices available I selected German and Geography rather than Chemistry and Physics. I was hopeless at Art and Woodwork: my marks were always below 30! This reduced my average marks substantially and as a result I never figured in the top 10 in the class. The situation when I reached Form5 was different since I dropped my weak subjects: this resulted in a much better average and I topped the class accordingly.

The main objective at the school was to prepare us for the Central Welsh Board examination, taken in the 5th year of school. A considerable proportion of the pupils did not enter these examinations, but chose (or were forced by family pressure to earn a living and contribute to family income) to leave at age 15 (later raised to 16). There was also the opportunity to matriculate: this meant passing at least 5 subjects, which had to include English, Mathematics, a Language, and Science.

As for me, just before CWB loomed I received a setback.

In 1948 I suffered a pleural effusion and was very ill for months. I was not able to return to school until the September of 1949 and I was now established in what for me was a new group of students. That year in Form 5 I excelled in most subjects, especially Maths and German. CWB had now been replaced by the Welsh Joint Education Committee exams and I succeeded in obtaining I had a very good WJEC certificate--3 Distinctions and 4 Credits. It meant I had matriculated and was qualified for further education. I was able to celebrate with others in my new Form 5.

It was in that year that I got very friendly with my dear friend Roy Lewis. We have been friends ever since. Unlike me, he was brilliant in English, but hopeless in Maths!

Sport and Song

During those years at Pentre Grammar it had not been all academic work of course. I made it into the school cricket XI under the captaincy of Ron Collins. In my final year at school I played with Tudor Edwards and Roy Lewis. I contributed to the team as a reliable spin bowler, and occasional fast-medium swing bowler, but I always recognised I was a better singer that a cricketer. I had been complimented and told I had a good soprano voice when singing in Hebron Chapel, and in the school choir (membership of which was virtually compulsory, to the chagrin of some of my fellow pupils). The choir practised in order to perform at the annual School Prizegiving held in Bethesda Chapel.

However things changed one year when I was in the process

of singing *Dafydd y Garrreg Wen*. My voice cracked. I thought my singing career was over but in reality it had hardly begun since Gladys Thomas, our music teacher, discovered that I now had a pleasing baritone voice. She persuaded me to compete in the 1949 St David's Day Eisteddfod at school (such competitions were held every year at the school, with prizes awarded for all academic subjects, and music including solos and group singing) That year I was awarded won first prize in the champion solo. I can't say the competing girls were very pleased at the result! My accompanying pianist was Derek Jones, whom I had known since Ton Boys School days. He eventually secured a music degree at Cardiff University. In later life he also performed as a pianist on various cruise ships.

I belonged to a family of committed Christians and we regularly attended Hebron Chapel just opposite Bethesda Chapel. Religious life in the Rhondda was supported by numerous such chapels: indeed, it was a notable fact that most of the bus stops in the valley were located outside chapels—or pubs! In 1949 Roy Lewis and I got together with a scheme: there was a short story writing competition held at the chapel so I got Roy to enter two stories under my name: he was ineligible to take part personally since he wasn't a member of the chapel. We won first prizes in the chapel eisteddfod: we shared the prize money. Not exactly ethical, perhaps, but we enjoyed spending the vouchers I was handed as a prize!

Conscription to the armed services had been introduced after the war for school leavers. National Service as it came to be called, was brought into legislation in 1947. The period of service was initially two years. All men aged 18 were liable to be called up but it was possible to defer service: this was allowed for university and college enrolments. Exemption completely could be claimed on medical grounds. Both Keith Roberts and I fell into this category, so we were excused from the call-up. Keith Lewis and Ken Wilkins were exempted because they had taken up reserved occupations, one in the pit and the other in the atomic power industry.

The Fifties and thereafter

There was no real system of careers advice at school: what advice was given tended to be very limited in scope, and given by a teacher who took it on reluctantly as a minor part of his work. It consisted mainly of handing out a few pamphlets, which were not particularly helpful. Most of my compatriots chose to leave school for work underground: the girls would mainly look for employment in shops or factories such as Polikoff's in Treorchy. For those who had matriculated the main options were to go on into the sixth form to prepare for university or college (an option taken up by very few) or to leave to seek employment, preferably of a white collar nature: banks, building societies, or public service, either in the valley or in Cardiff.

After the two years necessarily spent in the sixth form, and passing of the Higher School Certificate, application to university could be made. One year in the sixth form or employment was necessary before application to teacher training college could be entertained. Several girls such as Marilyn Davies, Pat Leyland and Mary Morris took that route and spent a year in the sixth.

I made the decision to opt for a college education to become a teacher. The profession in those days was held in considerable regard in the Rhondda. Probably because I was older than the others in Form 5 I had no need to go into the sixth form and consequently left school after matriculation in 1949. I secured a place in Caerleon College but still had to wait a year before entering. I was kicking my heels at home in this situation when, through a friend I heard of a three-month month vacancy in the Rhondda Council's Finance Department located in Pentre: I applied for the position, mainly as a stop-gap arrangement, and was appointed to the job.

The initial appointment was extended before I had finished the three months and I was then offered a junior post in the Education Finance Section of the Finance Department, which had been established when the Rhondda Council had been designated an Excepted District for Education under the Education Act 1944. Getting this post meant that my life changed considerably. It was not long before I gave up my intention of becoming a teacher—but I also discovered that my formal education was not to be regarded as completed. I was introduced to the tough examinations of the Institute of Municipal Treasurers and Accounts (later renamed, when it achieved a royal charter, as the Chartered Institute of Public Finance Accountants, or CIPFA for short.

While many courses of training for professional examinations were available in colleges such as Rhondda Technical College at that time, mostly on a part-time day release basis, no IMTA courses were on offer. Study had to by home preparation by way of correspondence courses. I signed for such a course with Alban and Lamb Newport. I faced the tough task of preparing for those professional examinations at home, in the evenings after work and at weekends. Keith Lewis meanwhile was undergoing the same agony, preparing in the evenings for membership of the Royal Institute of Chartered Surveyors after a day underground, while setting up his marital home with his newly acquired wife, Avril Owen from Kenry Street, Tonypandy.

It was four years later that, feeling reasonably secure financially I followed in his footsteps. I married Beti Davies, a fellow member of Hebron Chapel who worked as a librarian in Pentre. We socialised a great deal with Ken and Margaret who kept a newsagent shop in Ton. They were our best friends; they died in the 90s. We always went on holidays together (Ken had been my best man) and since Ken was a brilliant pianist the hotel management often asked us to perform: Ken at the piano and me singing. They offered us free holidays if we would perform (we never took up the offer) and even cancelled their visiting artists since they were impressed with our performances.

Initially, we moved in with Beti's parents when we got married. When our daughter Janet was born in 1958 in Glyncornel House in Llwynypia, we looked for other accommodation, and settled on No.9 Victoria Street. It was a financial struggle of course: my parents were kind enough to lend us some money—they were then still living in Rees

Street—and the price of £1,200 was paid. Our second daughter was also born in Victoria Street, in 1961 and in 1965, with my financial situation improving it was time to move again: this time to grander premises, the detached house at 18 St David's Street in Ton.

The house was called "Dolwen": on the one side were the grounds of St David's Church with its long gravelled drive, green sward and a profusion of rhododendron bushes. The house had been built by Alfred Bundy, who had worked as the manager of Ton Pit. I was amused to note that the plans for the house read "Villa for Alfred Bundy Esq". At the side of the house away from the church grounds there was an unmade-up lane, leading up past Wyndham Street and Kennard Street. It was used by the miners coming off shift—walking home to their houses at the valley floor. It provided a perfect location for Mr Bundy to keep an eye open on the workers, monitoring their time-keeping! They had to come down the lane between No 17 and 18 to reach their homes. Beti and I paid £3,750 for the house and have lived in it ever since.

A Sporting Life

I was recently honoured by honorary membership of the Barbarians Bowls Association. This was given in recognition of my involvement at the top level with star players in the world of bowls. This pleased me immeasurably: I was extremely proud of the honour. But how did it all start?

The mining community valued activity in the open air: it was the opportunity for working miners to breathe freely away from the thick, dusty, dangerous air of the pits. Many miners worked garden allotments, some kept racing pigeons, others played football (there were soccer clubs in Ton Pentre and Cwmparc but many other minor clubs such as the Tuesday League) and a large group played rugby: there were clubs in Ystrad, Treorchy, Treherbert and Blaenrhondda. But my father and uncle spent their leisure time in the open air playing bowls: it began as a leisure pursuit but became a family passion. Influenced by their enthusiasm my brother and I took up the game.

One of the great advantages of bowls is that, like cricket, you can have a long playing career—not possible in team sports like rugby and soccer. We started young, Mal and I: he was just 8 and I was 14 when we played our first game of bowls in Gelli Park. Since we came from what may be described as a bowling family Mal and I were early enthusiasts, much influenced by my mother's brother, my uncle John Morgan Evans. As for my father Cliff, he was reckoned by many to be the best uncapped bowler in Wales. He and Uncle John Morgan were a huge inspiration. They together won the Welsh pairs championship in 1952, and Uncle John became an international bowler, playing for Wales in that same year. Spurred on by his example, Mal and I were to follow in his footsteps, and even go further in the game.

In such a family environment it was perhaps inevitable that Mal and I were quickly "hooked" on the game .As youngsters we never bothered going to the beach like other lads; we preferred watching our uncle and father playing in bowls tournaments in Gelli Park and elsewhere. Consequently neither of us learned how to swim—but we learned the skills necessary for outdoor bowls from watching and playing and eventually became keen and proficient bowlers at the highest level.

Like me, Mal went to Ton Infants, Ton Boys School and entered Pentre Grammar School. He won a place at University College of Wales at Bangor and graduated in History in 1961. After completing a teacher training course in Cardiff he obtained a teaching post at Townhill, Swansea, before moving on to teaching posts in Porth and Tonypandy. He finally became a headmaster at Ferndale Secondary School.

Meanwhile he had become an iconic figure in the world of bowls. He continued playing at the Gelli Park Club with me, my father and uncle. Mal came to the sport's attention when he was just 17: the competition was played at Pontypridd and he won against a South African of note and reputation: Hugh Hughes. The next highlight was a competition played at Weston Super Mare, where he trounced the holder of the trophy. Headlines in the *Western Mail* read *Bowls Babe Beats Trophy Holder*!

During the next decade he consolidated his reputation and in 1956 he was selected to play for Wales. In the same year he was chosen to compete in the inaugural World Championships at which he succeeded in winning 12 out of 15 games to take the world title He recorded a comfortable 21-6 win over David Bryant. Oddly enough, Mal never won the Welsh national singles championsip, although he did succeed in winning the Gibson-Watt Welsh Open Singles at Llandrindo Wells in 1964, 1966 and 1967.But he and I took the national pairs championship in consecutive years in 1966 and 1967. Mal went on to become a major figure in the game, widely respected by his opponents. He also supported both the indoor and outdoor games as a selector and committee man.

As for me, I was at Mal's side in many tournaments and in fact we held a unique position: we were the only two brothers to achieve major honours in bowls. During the sixties we together competed in and won many open bowls tournaments. On two occasions in that era we were crowned Welsh Pairs champions, in the sixties. But our run of joint success came to a sad end in 2009, when Mal died. He was then 72 years of age and living in Upper Canning Street, Ton Pentre. He had been ill for a long time. It was a great blow for me, we had enjoyed such success together, and his wife Mary, whom he had married in 1967 deeply suffered his loss: she died shortly after his passing. But he left an enduring legacy as an historic figure in the game. Gareth, Mal's son carried on the tradition for a while: he became a junior Welsh Bowls international.

When I received the letter from the Welsh Bowling Association informing me of my own selection for Wales in the third position of one of the 5 Welsh Rinks I was thrilled. It justified the time and practice over many years The year was 1967, when I was aged 36—it was the beginning of a period when Beti could legitimately describe herself as a "bowls widow". She has borne the condition without complaint for many years!

My first game in the British Championships was in 1967: it was played at Llandarcy Swansea. I had a good series and was promoted to skip in the last game against the star Scottish Skip

Charlie Craig. To my delight, I won by 4 shots. From that point on I developed my game considerably I won the Porthcawl, Rhondda and National tournaments at both singles and pairs. This resulted in Welsh trials which led me to be chosen to represent Wales. I played in the Dundee Champion of Champions tournament and was then selected as captain of the Welsh team, playing at home and abroad. All prize money received was by way of vouchers!

I had won many open singles competitions by the time that the Commonwealth Games in 1978 were announced. They were to be held in Edmonton, Canada. A Welsh team was selected to take part—there were just 7 of us—and I played at skip for the Welsh Fours. We were kitted out in red and green blazers, and red sweaters adorned with the three feathers of Wales. I was put in charge of a section of the opening parade, so when I saw Lord Swansea, who was one of the shooting team and a Provincial Grand Master of Freemasonry, taking photographs, I spoke sharply to him that it wasn't allowed. He didn't enjoy the reprimand! But later at my lodge he installed our new Master he recognized me, with a friendly wink.

The competition itself was fiercely fought and we came home with a third place. But I was able to mount the rostrum to receive a bronze Medal.

In that same year I won the Welsh Singles Indoor title and was then appointed as captain of the Wales team to compete, once again in Australia, at Frankston near Melbourne in 1980. A business contact had provided us with new navy blazers and natty trilbies. We took the long, exhausting flight from

Heathrow and once arrived in Frankston, where we were staying, we had the opportunity to mingle with the other competitors: it was an occasion for making friends around the world. Taking part in the opening parade was a colourful, fantastic experience. It was a tight tournament with 20 nations taking part. We played every country on a round robin basis. The schedule demanded commitment from the whole team: we ended up by spending 12 hours a day on the green! I became friendly at that time with Peter Reuben of Australia. He said that he trained harder to play international bowls than playing Rugby--I believe he had played rugby for Australia.

The greens in Australia are much quicker than in the United Kingdom so we took some time to adjust to the different conditions. Our final match against Fiji ended in a draw, but we had managed to beat the home nation—Australia—and so came 5th in the tournament. We had only missed out on a medal because of a very close loss against Israel: they pipped us 15-14.

It was not all bowls, of course. In Melbourne I was invited to attend a function at a Masonic Lodge and was requested to provide entertainment to the brethren at the after proceedings by singing songs from the shows. Also, as captain of the Welsh team I was interviewed by a reporter from the *Melbourne Herald*. The interviewer asked me about my singing and I replied that singing when I played bowls helped my concentration and determination: I felt it was then I was at my most dangerous.

The next day the article appeared with rather a different

slant: the heading proclaimed *GORGEOUS GWYN LORD OF THE RINKS WITH MANY FEMALE FOLLOWERS!*

I admit I was always bit of a show man on the green especially against well known opposing skips, and maybe this appealed to Australian female followers of the game! Someone arranged for Beti to receive news of this article. Consequently, when I rang her ...well, you can imagine her reaction! In truth, however, the family was delighted with the article.

I should add that the game of bowls is more serious than many would believe, particularly those youngsters who feel it's a game for old men. There are strict rules, but as in all sports there is the matter of gamesmanship. It can help you get out of a tight spot if you can distract your opponent.

I once skipped a four against an English skip in one series. The jack (or kitty in bowls parlance) must be at least 25 metres from the edge of the mat that you are standing on. I liked my players to play short jacks and I'd got to the situation where I was really hammering the English skip, I was up 15 nil on 6 ends in a game which comprises 21 ends. The English skip tried to break our concentration by asking me to agree that he could leave the green to go to the toilet.

I agreed.

Then, when he returned after his comfort break I responded in like manner: I asked him the same question. He was, of course, unable to refuse. So off I went in my turn and his ploy had rebounded upon him. We ended up beating him 26-7.

A lot of tricks of this kind were played at top level. I loved the tension and essential playfulness of it all but I recognised that some of my colleagues had difficulty coping with the pressure.

My own personal manner of dealing with such pressure was in itself distracting to opponents: it was a regular practice of mine to challenge my opponents' jacks even if I really knew the jacks were up legally.

I always regarded this as fair in tight games especially if your players were having a bad game. Basically it was all about trying to break your opponent's "Rhythm". Some opposing players in my experience would even deliberately move to put off opponents standing on the mat and about to deliver the bowl: a smooth delivery of the bowl is crucial when stepping off the mat!

And I know that my opponents were often puzzled and distracted by the fact that when I found myself in a tricky situation I would concentrate by quietly singing from my repertoire of songs from the shows.

As I mentioned earlier, it was on these occasions—when I was indulging in my two passions at the same time—that I could be most dangerous!

Looking back over the years, it gives me a warm feeling that I've made so many friends in the bowling world: I'm still in contact with some far-flung friends like Errol Bungey in Australia and Frank De Souza in California. And I got to appear on television.

My first appearance was at the HTV studios in Cardiff along with Mal, David Bryant and David Rhys Jones. I enjoyed considerable personal success on this occasion. We played on a short green and I won four gold plated goblets. Then in 1979 I travelled to Coatbridge in Scotland with the great David Bryant for the first televised indoor bowls tournament—with a first prize of 5 goblets. David Bryant won the tournament and I came 4th—receiving a medal and an inscribed glass decanter. Times have changed now, of course. In the 90s the game went professional, indoor bowls was televised regularly and prizes changed from glass goblets to cash: first prizes of £5,000.

But all good things come to an end. I retired in 1995, debilitated by arthritic knees. But I can proudly boast that in my career I was never dropped from the Welsh team.

So there it is: I had come a long way from playing bowls with tennis balls in a dirty stony back lane at the rear of a terraced house in Gelli, to playing bowls at the highest level on the fastest greens in the world.

I owe a great deal to my club Gelli Park: the club was the greatest team in Wales in the 70s and 80s having won the national club completion on 4 occasions and runners up on 3 occasions. Remarkably at one time there were 9 capped players in a team of 16.

Touring with the Wales team brought together a group who became close friends and I was able to bring together my two skills and pleasures: I was regularly called upon to sing in the evenings on tour. It was a matter of selecting songs from the well-known musicals of the day.

In particular the requests were often to sing songs from the musical *South Pacific:* the song *Some Enchanted Eve*ning was a regular request, as was *If I Loved You* from *Carousel*. It was all a long way from Gelli Park!

And there is my long-suffering family: I can never express adequately my gratitude for the support they have ungrudgingly given during my sporting career.

But my active involvement in the game ended in 2014: I was forced to retire, forced out by pain from arthritic knees. But I had enjoyed great years and my international travels led to my making numerous friends in the bowling world.. Japan Australia New Zealand Papua New Guinea, among others.

But it was not all about sport, of course: I had a professional career to follow in addition.

Professional progression

I had started at the Rhondda Council in Pentre in October 1949 as temporary junior clerk in the Finance Department: most of my work being connected with the Sundry Debtors-Rates Ledger. In March of the following year, I had become a permanent clerk and was promoted to Education Finance Assistant. This necessitated a move: instead of being located in Pentre I now found myself working in Bronwydd House, a train ride away at Porth. Bronwydd House had been purchased by the council for £10,000. While I was there I started studying for IMTA examinations.

Mal holding the Pairs Championship Cup

IMTA had started life as the Corporate Treasurers' and Accountants' Institute in 1885. It was renamed the Institute of

Municipal Treasurers and Accountants (IMTA) in 1901. This later became the Chartered Institute of Public Finance and Accountancy (CIPFA) in 1973 when it finally obtained its Royal Charter.

Concentrating mainly upon my daytime employment I found it took me 4 years before I was able to sit the first IMTA exam. It wasn't just a matter of Accounts, of course: one of the main textbooks I had to study was a well-regarded textbook, Steven' *Mercantile Law*. More to the point as far as my career was concerned was Hart's *Local Government Law*. These were text books which were used in universities, the Bar and other professional body examinations.

The correspondence course meant that I was called to study the texts supplied, then complete tests which were sent away for marking. When I felt confident enough, and had done enough preparatory work I decided it was time to attempt the Intermediate exam. It was 1953 and I was delighted to find that I had passed: I was one of a relatively small group--only 62 candidates were successful in the country at that time.

My examination success was recognized by promotion. There was nothing clearly available for me at that time in Rhondda Borough Council Finance department so I applied for, and was appointed to the post of assistant accountant in the County Treasurer's Dept Cardiff. It meant a long day, travelling from the Rhondda by train from Ystrad down to Cardiff, though fortunately there was a regular hourly service.

My salary increased from £160 per annum to £500 a year. .But all was not roses. In my new environment it was not just a matter of settling in: I went through psychological hell for the first 6 months. The problem was the chief accountant: in my view he was an unmitigated swine who made his dislike of valley boys quite clear. However the experience and the slights endured during his tyrannical rule did me good and helped me learn to stand on my own two feet.

So I grew in confidence. I was responsible in those days, *inter alia* for the accounts of Small Holdings and the Fire Service .But there were further examinations to pass until I was properly qualified and further correspondence courses to plough through. I had settled into married life by then, and I passed my two final exams by 1957. I had achieved my objective: I was now a professionally qualified accountant.

The next step, now I was fully qualified was to seek further promotion: this came when I secured posts of auditor and accountant in Cardiff City Council. One important task allocated to me in those days was to deal with the capital financing of the Wales Empire Pool (now closed of course). I also audited the accounts of all of the City's establishments.

I enjoyed the responsibilities laid upon me during my years in Cardiff but I was still looking for opportunities that might arise back in the Rhondda Borough Council. So now, as a qualified public finance accountant I returned to employment in the Rhondda with relief in 1958: The appointment was that of Assistant Treasurer, mainly dealing with committee estimates and the Rate Levy. Among other matters I also dealt with the council's loan debt ensuring that all short term loans were carrying the lowest interest rates in the market. Saving taxpayers' money!

In the 60s disaster struck the Rhondda: there was a virulent outbreak of smallpox and outsiders were advised to avoid the valley. Beti's brother Ben contracted the disease and died in the 1960s from the smallpox injection. There were lines of people waiting for vaccination (including me and all my family) and there was a terrible feeling of isolation as travel to and out of the Rhondda was restricted. The Penrhys Isolation hospital was eventually closed after treating several patients: the consultant died from the disease. At that time I was Assistant Treasurer and I can remember how worried our Public Health Officers were.. Nor was it the only disaster of the time: at one point Rees Street, Smith Street and Lloyd Street were inundated by floods as the river banks burst after heavy rain, and we had the unusual sight of boats being ferried along the roads and streets to bring food and other assistance to beleaguered families—delivered through upstairs windows! The banks were finally reinforced and strengthened—but only after innumerable council meetings and discussion of the financial implications.

I held the post of Assistant Treasurer for 9 years—no more daily train rides to Cardiff—and it in 1967 I was appointed Deputy Treasurer in 1967. I was to hold that position for six years.

The senior position in local authorities in those days was designated as Town Clerk. By long tradition the situation was always held by a qualified lawyer, usually a solicitor who had spent his career after qualifying legally in local government service. But when Local Government Reorganisation was ushered in during 1973 the title of Town Clerk was discarded.

Chief Executive

More importantly for me, the position was rendered open to a wider range of candidates and for the first time the post was renamed Chief Executive. This applied in most councils

My main professional objective had previously been—a distant banner to aim for if you like—to become a Borough Treasurer and sign cheques in that capacity. That had been the extent of my ambition, but now a different, more important opportunity was at hand. I had developed a good relationship with elected members of the council and some of them now encouraged me to make application for the new post of Chief Executive. I had nothing to lose, so applied. I was successful, and was appointed in that year of reorganisation—at the magnificent salary of £7,300.

I was somewhat embarrassed by the fact that my management team included my old boss, but he retired soon afterwards which made life a bit easier.

The job I had won was eventually given the sonorous, rolling title of Chief Executive, Head of Paid Service and Monitoring Officer and I worked in that capacity until I retired in 1994. I enjoyed every moment especially being in charge of all elections. Over that period I installed 20 Mayors and of course attended with Beti all 20 Civic dinners. In 1988 I had heard that Roy Lewis had been elected President of the Chartered Secretaries Institute so I invited him as guest speaker at one of them, in 1988, and it was a thrill for me to see my old school friend performing.

During my period as Chief Executive I was presented to most of the Royal Family and attended a garden Party at Buckingham Palace. During the Queen's visit to Caerphilly Castle I was also presented with a silver Jubilee medal.

Some further appointments came my way after retirement.

In 1994 I was appointed by the Secretary of State for Wales as a member of the Rhondda Health Trust. I became Deputy Chairman, and Chair of the Audit Committee and Remuneration Committee. I was also invited to chair mental health hearings in what was then the East Glamorgan Hospital. I served in this capacity until 1999. Bernard Jones, the Management Director of BUY AS YOU VIEW was also a member. Gareth George, another Pentre Grammar boy was also on the Board. He was a very highly placed Director in Barclays Bank Wayne Thomas a solicitor in Treorchy was also involved.

I also kept myself busy by setting up as a self-employed accountant in my late son-in-law's office in Ynyshir .He was an insurance agent, who died in 2009.

Most of my clients during this period were sole traders and partnerships. My qualification as a member of CIPFA did not permit me to deal with companies, but I was able to work as an independent auditor of Community Councils. I undertook this work for four such bodies. But it came to an end in 2016 when I finally retired from self-employment. I now have the leisure to look back over my working life and think again about the celebrities I met in the Mayor's Parlour at Rhondda, including Ken Dodd, Mat Monroe and Michael Ball. One of the mayors , Annie Powell, was a Communist, rather than the usual Labour supporter, and she invited the Russian Ambassador to the parlour on one occasion. He presented me with a gift—Russian caviar!   That's what I call living high on the hog!

All has not been wine and roses, of course.

Beti and I had two daughters Janet and Susan, and in due course three grandchildren arrived: Christopher, Aled and Laura, and also three great grand children Deon, Regan and Emilia.

But there have been tribulations as well: Aled developed leukemia at 5 and consequently we went through an agonising period in our lives. Aled survived however, after a successful bone transplant. There was also the blow of the death at an early age of my son-in-law.

Aled is now 30 and works in the Library Service but his treatment has left him with many health problems.

Chris went to Swansea University and secured an honours degree in Sports Science but then followed in my footsteps by working in public service, for the enlarged authority Rhondda Cynon Taf, as an Information Technology advisor in the Education Dept.

My own love of song has been reflected in the career of my dear grand-daughter, Laura. After achieving an Honours Degree in Musical Theatre at Mount View Academy in London she took to the stage. She has done remarkably well, a diva who has worked with celebrities such as Jason Donovan in musical theatres throughout the United Kingdom and America. But she shows the strength of Rhondda roots—she retains a home in Ton Pentre.

Nowadays I have time to reflect how I've been blessed with a wonderful wife Beti: though at present she is very ill, for over 62 years we've enjoyed life with our two lovely daughters, three grand-children and three beautiful great-grand children. During Beti's illness I have been provided with immense support from my son-in-law, Stephen, who has proved to be a rock. I'm grateful for these blessings, and for the long-time friendships which were formed.

Commonwealth blazer with family fans

DEWI GRIFFITHS

I WENT TO SEE my GP the other day and he gave me the diagnosis that I am suffering a form of narcolepsy—I'm sleepy and listless during the day but wide awake at night. Probably the result of the schedules I kept during my sixty years working for the BBC!

I live in Tongwynlais now with my daughter, with grandchildren close by but I was born in Wyndham Street, Ton Pentre in the Rhondda. I well recall my first visit to Tongwynlais: it was about 1950 and the history master at Pentre Grammar School brought a group of us down by train to Taffs Well, then we climbed up the mountain, to have matters of historical interest pointed out to us, such as ancient tumuli, before coming down to bathe in Taffs Well natural pool—long since gone. We then enjoyed a lemonade in the pub, and a pie—too young to drink alcohol, not with a teacher sitting beside you.

But the Rhondda was my early home and I look back to my childhood and youth in Ton Pentre with affection—apart from the streets, the mountain was our playground, the golf course known as the *Waun* being one day the Wild West where we rode imaginary horses and killed Indians, another day the Sahara Desert, where we battled with the wild Riff tribesmen—much of our background inspiration being gleaned from the films we saw in the Workmen's Hall cinema in Ton. The old putting greens on the *Waun* later served as areas where we could play touch rugby without scarring our knees too much.

Then there was Forgione's ice-cream cart travelling from street to street, a colourful, gaily painted two-wheeler drawn by a somewhat dejected pony, Sunday school trips to Aberavon through the tunnel at Blaencwm, learning about girls…they are days I look back to with nostalgia: a different, gentler time, at least until the advent of the Second World War.

The Thirties

I was born on August 16 1931 in Wyndham Street, Ton Pentre, close by to a boy who emerged into the light of day about the same time. Leighton Brunt was one of my early playmates and was to become a lifelong friend. My father, Bryn, like most other men in Ton Pentre worked in the pit until he contracted "dust" and was invalided out of the industry. .He was a quiet, somewhat reserved man but my mother, commonly known as Jinnie, was quite the opposite: vivacious, a great honky tonk piano player who cut hair as a sideline. Genes being what they are I guess my brother Billie took after my father, while I inherited my mother's love of entertainment. Never did take up hair-cutting, though.

When I was about six years old we moved up the hill from Wyndham Street to Kennard Street, to live directly opposite Roy Lewis. I remember his father Harold well: his large allotment was bounded by a blackberry hedge and when we went blackberrying, pulling at the hedge, he'd sometimes emerge from the house, snarling and growling at us. But there was always a twinkle in his eye as he did so.

On August 30, 1937 I was six years old but my father allowed me and my brother Bill to stay up into the early hours for a momentous occasion—Tommy Farr was fighting Joe Louis for the world championship. A number of people gathered around our wireless set that night to listen to the broadcast from the Yankee Stadium. Born in Clydach, nicknamed the Tonypandy Terror, Tommy Farr was not expected to win: Louis had knocked out his eight previous opponents, and went on the similarly dispatch the next seven after the Farr fight. But Tommy attacked the Black Bomber fiercely and hurt him: the fight went the full distance of 15 rounds.

The occasion was one of great excitement: the older boys staying up with us ran the length of the street at intervals, taking turns to tell the surface workers at the Maindy Colliery pithead of Tommy's progress at the end of each round, so the news could be sent down the shaft telephone to those working at the coal face. The following Saturday we were able to watch the action on the newsreel at the Workmen's Hall.

When the referee awarded the fight to Joe Louis the Stadium resounded to booing of 50,000 fans: it was regarded as a controversial decision. One British sportswriter commented that the referee's decision was "... that of a man either blindly partisan or afflicted with astigmatism. It is a verdict that justifies the belief that nothing short of the annihilation of Louis would have given Farr victory."

Thirty years later I had the privilege of sharing those memories with Tommy Farr when as a BBC TV Sports producer I made a programme about his career in the ring, as he chatted with Alun Williams in the studio, a former vestry at the lower end of Sapphire Street. The reminiscences went on well past midnight, back in the bar of his hotel.

With Cliff Morgan in the studio

We were not in Kennard Street long before my father was presented with a different opportunity: he applied for and was appointed Librarian and Manager of the Workman's Hall in Ton. It meant that for the rest of my young life I resided on the premises and in some ways it changed my life.

Like others in the streets I started my education young, going to the infants school in Gelli, a short downhill walk from Kennard Street. There I found myself sitting alongside Leighton Brunt, Gwyn Evans, Jack Hodder, youngsters who were to remain my friends all my life.

The Forties

My father Bryn always had an interest in radio and was prescient enough to photograph me, in 1934, wearing headphones: a hint towards my future career! He took to repairing wireless receivers after he left the pit until he was appointed Librarian and manager of the Maindy and Eastern Workman's Hall and Institute, (The Works) .This proved to be a boon as far as I was concerned because since the building included a cinema I was able to see just about every film that came out of Hollywood as a youngster during the forties, as well as listening avidly to the radio. Tommy Handley in *ITMA, Monday Night at Eight*... And the BBC seemed almost central to my early existence: when they built BBC Broadcasting House, a photograph of it went up in our home in the Rhondda. I thought that was like Westminster Cathedral, it had this awesome effect. The family wireless was hardly ever switched off and a day at home was never without the sound of the Dance Bands on the BBC. With a piano in the living room on which my mother would play the popular songs of the time, I grew up with a wide knowledge of the songs and singers of what is often referred to as 'The Golden Age of Entertainment'.

Shortly afterwards the war years followed, and family life centred around war reports on the wireless. As a young lad I soon came to recognise the distinctive sounds of the enemy aircraft. I suppose my intense interest in World War Two began on day one – 3rd September 1939, when, at the age of eight, I sat with my brother Bill, who was then 12, and my mother in the living room of our home in Wyndham Street. My father insisted we all listen to the wireless as he tuned in for a special bulletin from London. The announcer introduced the prime minister , Neville Chamberlain, who spoke to us directly from the Cabinet Room at 10 Downing Street, and he ended with these chilling words: "Consequently this country is at war with Germany".

That battery-powered wireless never seemed to be switched off after that. Every day, from September 1939 to August 1945, I heard all about the progress of the war - a conflict accurately described as "a world war". Initially, the reports were all about the BEF—the British Expeditionary Force arriving in France to help the French in their fight against the rapidly advancing German army, but Hitler's Panzer Divisions were strong and well-prepared. The combined British and French forces were no real match, and so, by the spring of 1940, I was listening to reports about what was described as "the miracle of Dunkirk" when a third of a million allied soldiers were taken off the beaches in thousands of little boats to be taken to the safety of the south of England. Those were the days when the dreaded word "invasion" became part of every-day conversation.

It was at another family gathering when we all gathered around the wireless as my father switched on to listen to the new prime minister, Winston Churchill, and it was then we heard his historic pronouncement: "The Battle of France is over. I expect that the Battle of Britain is about to begin." The speech ended with a typical "Winnie" rallying statement: "if the British Empire and its Commonwealth last for a thousand years, men will still say, this was their finest hour!"

Our other source of information was of course, the newspapers, with the London dailies issuing maps of the south coast, pinpointing the places which were being bombed by the Luftwaffe providing the first reports that citizens had been killed. The newspapers also began issuing leaflets with "aircraft recognition silhouette charts", and by my ninth birthday, in the middle of August, I was able to identify various enemy airplanes such as Junkers, Dornier and Fokke-Wulf and Messerschmidt. Billie and I were also aware of the different sound made the engines of a German bomber - an oscillating drone produced by the different engine rotation speeds resulting in a distinctive "beat" frequency.

But we were far away from the actual danger at that time. Cardiff was targeted, of course, but the arrival of bombs in the valley was limited: Cwmparc was bombed, and there was a stray bomb dropped near Gelli Colliery but that was about it. The years of the Depression were over with the advent of war and employment possibilities grew apace: the coal and steel industries stepped up production, and buses took hundreds of women from the valley every day to work in the munitions factories in the Vale of Glamorgan. In Ton Pentre the Pictorium Cinema, in Albion Street, just down the hill from Kennard and Wyndham Streets, was converted to serve as a munitions factory.

There were regular reports during the Battle of Britain by BBC reporters referring to battles between German fighters and RAF pilots as "dog fights" - which was when I first heard about the icon of my wartime years - the Spitfire. At the time I wondered what it looked like, because we youngsters were kept busy otherwise with gas mask drill, air raid precautions, and getting to know the strangers amongst us: the evacuees who had arrived from London, the Midlands, and later the docklands of Cardiff.

As for entertainment, during those years there was the Saturday morning "rush" - the local cinema putting on special entertainment films for children - and it was at the Workmen's Hall in Ton Pentre that I first saw a Spitfire in flight, in the newsreel that came up between *Hopalong Cassidy* and *Donald Duck*. From the moment I saw it on that big screen I was fired with an ambition to be a pilot in the RAF. The newsreel coverage of the dog fights caused more excitement among the youngsters than anything Hollywood could conjure up.

The Battle of Britain was central to our existence at that period. When father came up from the night shift at the local colliery, the first thing he always asked about was "are we winning the battle?" After hearing the news and before jumping into the tin bath in front of the fire he would make his way across to the allotments at the end of Kennard and Wyndham street where he would spend time tending to the vegetable patch and checking if there were any eggs in the chicken coop.

And that's how it was. Day after day, hour after hour, we listened to the radio for reports, such as: "Early this morning eight German planes were shot down over Kent - six of our aircraft failed to return to base!" Billy and I kept track of these events by posting a chart on the wall where we put a cross on emblems of a Union Jack or a swastika. It was also fascinating to us to hear that the pilots defending our homeland were not just British, but came from all over the Commonwealth, and from the occupied countries in Europe. There was a significant number of Poles serving in the RAF. As September came, we heard that Churchill had supplied the RAF with more aircraft, and more importantly, replacement pilots.

As a nine-year-old I didn't know what the word "propaganda" meant, but I was aware that the news bulletins were telling us that more and more German aircraft were being shot down - and that the end was in sight. The end? Hardly that! In September 1940 the war had hardly touched us in the valley, but we were fully aware that the people residing in the south of England had been living through hell. Then came the radio announcement - the strangest report for months:"For the last 24 hours there have been no reports of any German aircraft in the skies over England." So, they were right! The end was in sight. At least the threat of invasion had been repelled: an occasion for celebration!

School Days

After a year in Bronllwyn (the system had decreed that I would not be successful in the 11+ examinations) I did well enough to be selected to go to the grammar school in Pentre, where I met up again with former friends such as Gwyn Evans. Those were days when I was constantly breaking my glasses (often with the assistance of an awkwardly bouncing rugby ball), driving my mother to distraction. It meant I usually had to sit in the front row of the class—in order to be able to read the blackboard. Ron Kinsey was similarly myopic: we sometimes sat next to each other and shared a single, somewhat battered pair of glasses. It caused comment. But it worked as a system.

Bindles Night Club, Barry
Back row: Roy, Leighton, Dewi, Brian with partners
Foreground Ralph & Eileen Meredith

I became active in the School Club, to which Forms 3 and above were welcomed for evening activities once a week. It was not very active but I managed to introduce some new techniques. I had access to a tape recording machine (not very many around in those days) and I recall drafting Mansel Lloyd in to assist me: the assembly hall at the school (which also served as a gymnasium) had some classrooms leading off it and while I set up a microphone on the hall stage Mansel linked up the system in one of the classrooms, and we got members of the audience to come up, make a contribution into the mike, and after it was over Mansel would play back the recording to the audience. I was very surprised one evening when someone balked at performing and Roy Lewis volunteered to take his place. He sang *"Temptation"* and I accompanied him on the piano. It ended in a right racket! There was also the group pulled together to sing a spoof of Bing Crosby's hit song *"Blue Skies"* in a *Spike Jones and his City Slickers* style. Ken Wilkins's main role was to make a tongue clicking noise when I pretended to shoot down a buzzing fly but he had to do it several times, in growing desperation, because the audience laughter at our antics drowned out his contribution. It had a good reception also when some of us spent a week in Dyffrin, on a sixth form course a year or so later. I had started out on my production and directing career!

Occasionally Mansel and I used his tape recorder in the basement at home, recording plays I had written and using my friends as performers. One of them was a zany production; I had written the script and used any background sound devices we could dig up: Roy Lewis's contribution to one was a brief dramatic track from Rimsky Korsakoff's *Scheherazade* while to the background noise of a Tube train Leighton Brunt could be heard pronouncing the immortal words "Mind the doors, please!"

In later years, like me Mansel also joined the BBC and became a producer of the TV show *Tonight* and other current affairs programmes, working with Cliff Michelmore. He also did a stint with Yorkshire television.

Jack, Dewi.Leighton, Mansel & sisters Jean and Mary Parry

And of course there was also the rugby. I played for the school team—there were matches against other grammar schools in Ferndale, Quakers Yard, Tonypandy, Tonyrefail, Porth County and Porth Grammar (where Leighton Brunt starred) among others. Sometimes the girls' hockey team travelled with us on a hired bus to the venue: always occasions for a bit of rowdyism! The leading players at hockey were Pat Leyland and Enid Benbow, who became good friends. I also turned out for Treorchy Boys Club, along with Keith Lewis and Roy Lewis— and on one occasion, Gareth Griffiths, who insisted on playing at wing forward instead of his usual position of centre or wing (in which positions he later played for Wales and the British Lions).

It was in that period that I indulged my interest in performing by entering a Go as You Please competition—they were held on the stages of theatre-cinemas in the valleys—to start an act based on one of the eccentric Hollywood film personalities of the day: the ebullient Danny Kaye who starred in such films as *Holiday Inn* with Bing Crosby.

Danny Kaye's forté lay in delivering packed lyrics with a frenzied articulation of his limbs and contortions of his features. It was all very quick-fire: in a number from the film *Lady in the Dark* he managed to reel off the names of 100 Russian composers in 38 seconds.

I studied his performances closely in the darkness of the cinema in the Institute until I got his mannerisms off word—and action—perfect. I appeared on the stage with a recording of his songs playing behind the curtain while I mimed to the audience.

I won the competition, and started a brief career on various stages as *The Welsh Danny Kaye*.

The Fifties
The family respect for the BBC stayed with me. After leaving school, I headed on to national service with the Royal Air Force. While Leighton Brunt was sent off to Aden, I was posted to Luneberg in Germany—where he would have loved to be posted. The armed forces really did not know what to do with us—it was suggested I could work as a cook but when I asked to work as a technician I was told I would have to sign on for three years, instead of the usual two. I signed on and was consequently employed usefully, unlike many other national

servicemen. My decision to sign on for the extra years paid off in terms of experience: I was put to working on radar which only stimulated my interest in the entertainment business.. During my three years with the Royal Air Force I became a member of a small jazz group, playing the piano and the saxophone and performing with my imitations of famous Hollywood musical stars, such as, inevitably, Danny Kaye, I was given the honour of becoming the opening act of The RAF Revue Show.

On saxophone at RAF Show, Luneberg

Sport

Sport was always an important fact of life in the armed forces but there was no rugby team at RAF Luneberg when I arrived so I busied myself in forming a rugby XV and became the skipper of the side. But as my RAF career drew to a close I took a deep breath and wrote to the BBC and asked them for a job. I was interviewed in May 1954, accepted and started working as Technical Assistant with the Welsh Home Service. In 1955 I found myself in Machynlleth snowed in as I undertook an outside broadcast.

That first job was described as Probationary Technical Assistant and it meant working in the control room and studio centre at Park Place, Cardiff, and Broadway Methodist Chapel, the home of the fledgling TV Wales service. There I was able to make full use of my experience as a Radar Technician during my RAF days. It was a useful start, learning the ropes, starting at the bottom! But two years later, in 1956 another opportunity came my way: I was able to transfer to television at the BBC TV building at Baynton House, Llandaff, the site of today's Broadcasting House. During this period I was able to pick up different skills and experiences which stood me in good stead later: I took up various roles: a Vision Engineer, a Cameraman, and a Sound Supervisor, balancing the microphones for outside broadcasts and the choirs and BBC Orchestra in the studio.

In 1961 there came a big opportunity: I was given the chance to become an Outside Broadcasting Stage Manager with Peter Dimmock's production team in London. It was a breakthrough that sharpened and extended my skills and when I returned to Wales at the end of 1962 it was to join the legendary Wales outside half, Cliff Morgan, the newly appointed Sports Organiser and Tom Davies, the radio producer, as BBC Wales formed its very own Sports Department.

Following Cliff's retirement from his sparkling career in the game in 1958 he had found a new career in broadcasting. Although he will forever be remembered for his celebrated commentary on the 1973 Barbarians rugby match against the touring All Blacks at Cardiff (particularly the commentary of "that golden try") his broadcasting career was far more wide-ranging and influential than that single event would suggest.

During his playing days he had already been spotted by the BBC in Wales as a natural talker and communicator, and in 1960, at the invitation of the BBC's Head of Welsh Programmes, Hywel Davies, he had joined BBC Wales as Sports Organiser in Cardiff. His exceptional ability as a programme-maker and story-teller briefly took him outside the familiar world of BBC Sport in the mid-1960s, when he spent two years as editor of ITV's current affairs programme *This Week*. Returning to the BBC he then produced and edited established TV sports programmes such as *Grandstand* and *Sportsnight* with David Coleman, and, from 1970, was himself one of the original team captains (opposite the former boxer Henry Cooper) on the long-running TV quiz *A Question of Sport*. In radio he found a natural outlet for his love of music, presenting for a time the BBC Radio 2 series *These You Have Loved*.

Later, Cliff rose to join the ranks of leading BBC executives. In 1974 he became Head of BBC Radio Sport and Outside

Broadcasts, and from 1976 to 1987 he was Head of BBC Television Sport and Outside Broadcasts, supervising coverage of major events including football World Cups, Commonwealth and Olympic Games, Royal weddings and other national ceremonial occasions, notably the funeral of Mountbatten in 1979 and the wedding of Charles and Diana in 1981.

My professional relationship with Cliff started when in 1962 the BBC decided to expand its TV coverage of sports. I found myself working alongside Cliff and radio producer Tom Davies. I'd known Cliff as a schoolboy, of course: he played for Tonyrefail Grammar School before joining Cardiff RFC and started his meteoric rise to become perhaps the best outside half in the UK. He, Tom Davies and I spent several years in the Sports department which was quickly expanded and I was recognised, as Mervyn Davies the legendary Welsh player put it in his biography, as an "up and coming young producer". Mervyn had been forced into retirement after a brilliant career for Wales and the Lions by a cerebral haemorrhage. I tried to get him started on a career with the BBC as a rugby pundit but sadly he didn't make the grade.

Cliff and I worked together for years. But in due course I was given a directorial role and I began directing coverage of rugby matches at the Cardiff Arms Park. In 1968 I was executive producer for the Lions tour in South Africa. I ended up directing the cameras at every rugby match played at Cardiff Arms Park for the next 30 years.

It wasn't just all about rugby, of course: I also worked on the BBC's other sports coverage. It was an exciting time, those early years at the BBC Sports department alongside Cliff and Onllwyn Brace. It meant international travel as the job took me all over the world. There was the coverage of six British Lions rugby tours where I was involved. The first was the 1966 tour of Australia and New Zealand. The team beat Australia twice but were whitewashed in New Zealand: it was a long tour—35 matches—at the end of which the players were exhausted. But for me, over the next few years it was great experience.

It was the Golden Era for Wales rugby and I was privileged to have a beer after the game with leading players of the day, such as Mervyn Davies, Bryn Meredith. Gerald Davies, JPR Williams, JJ Williams, Phil Bennett, and the inimitable Gareth Edwards. It culminated in 1987 when I was in Sydney, covering the inaugural Rugby World Cup.

Then there was the Olympic Games, and World Cup soccer. Although relationships between the professional game of rugby league and Welsh rugby union were, to put it bluntly, less than cordial that didn't mean coverage of league games fell outside my purview.

There were also other sports to cover for BBC Wales: horse racing, boxing, and golf. I also enjoyed covering 12 seasons of the tennis championships at Wimbledon. Among my standout memories of Wimbledon Final matches were the wins by Australian John Newcombe, and Australia's Yvonne Goolagong beating Billy Jean Moffat in July 1967. Moreover, my coverage of the quarter-final match between Britain's Roger Taylor, and South Africa's Cliff Drysdale launched the Colour Television Service of the BBC.

They were vintage years for me. I worked with most of the big sporting names of the day, from Scottish rugby union commentator Bill McLaren, England rugby captain Bill Beaumont and Australian tennis player Rod Laver. I stayed with the sports team until 1992.

I even managed to do a bit of teaching: I taught journalism in Palestine, for the Thomson Foundation.

Looking back over that thirty year period I realise I directed the cameras at every rugby match played at Cardiff Arms Park, the first being Wales v England in 1963. It was very different from the modern coverage: the programme was beamed live into *Grandstand*, but with only three cameras, no action replay and no zoom lenses. I remember well covering the 1966 Cardiff v Australia match and have particularly fond memories of The 'Golden Years' of the 1970s, not least when I covered the famous 1973 Barbarians defeat of the All Blacks, with Cliff Morgan providing the commentary. But I never forgot my early days in the Rhondda which was underlined by the chance to become friendly with Rhondda men who became stars of radio and Hollywood, such as Glyn and Donald Houston and Stanley Baker.

String of Pearls

It was a dazzling time but like all things it had to come to an end. My twilight career began when I was given the job of a BBC Radio Wales disc jockey. I say it was a *twilight* career but in fact it that lasted for more than twenty years. I had the idea of a weekly programme. a presentation of Golden Oldies music which had enthused me as a youngster in the Rhondda. The programme was first aired in the autumn of 1988, and as a new presenter, I came on air stating my credentials: a child of the Depression of the '30s, becoming a teenager during World War II, serving with the RAF during my National Service in the early '50s, and describing how along the way I became a huge fan of the BBC Dance Band Years, the Golden Age of Hollywood musicals, and the Big Band Era

How did it come about? Well, four years before I left sport coverage, I made a foray into this different kind of radio programming, and created a listenership for the sort of music I enjoyed myself. I went to the head of radio and said I had spent years trying to find a radio show I liked, playing the music I liked. She gave me a six-week spot to prove myself. The success of what became *A String of Pearls* is evidenced by its longevity, something which is traceable back to my sheer love for the subject matter. I never really enjoyed any music published after 1959, but that still left me with more than two million records to choose from! I was of course harking back to my youth: mostly in my teenage years it was listening to the American Forces Network, an influence that stayed with me as I did my show. You can guarantee so much of it was something I first learned and got excited about back in my teenage years.

The programme meant introducing original recordings of the songs and stars of yesteryear, indulging myself in the nostalgia of my formative years in the Workman's Hall, listening to all those old songs and watching all those vintage films. So that was how I was appointed as presenter of the hugely popular *'A String of Pearls'*, which I went on to broadcast every Sunday morning on Radio Wales. Thanks to the international appeal of the show, I would receive fan mail from all over the world. It would also not be uncommon for messages to come through from couples who have been married for 50 or 60 years, or more, hearing a song that was part of their early romantic life together.

One personally nostalgic programme was recorded at Treorchy Rugby Club. I had come across an old photograph of the 1948 Treorchy Boys Club XV, which included myself standing next to Gareth Griffiths, with in the front row Roy Lewis and Keith Lewis, who was captain. I conceived the idea of getting in touch with all the team members, and with the exception of Ken Elliott, who had played at scrum-half, the whole team turned up in Treorchy that evening for a group photograph (later published in the *Western Mail*) after which I interviewed each of them for the *String of Pearls* programme the following Sunday morning. Musical choices varied: Gareth Griffiths chose Nellie Lutcher's *Fine Brown Frame*, recalling dance evenings with his girl friend Pat Leyland at the Library in Tonypandy, while Roy Lewis chose *Cigareets and Whusky and Wild, Wild Women*. Didn't press him what memories were involved there!

Treorchy Boys Club RFC: front row 2nd left Roy Lewis, Keith Lewis centre (captain)
Second Row 4th left Dewi Griffiths, 5th left Gareth Griffiths.

The evening ended with a few beery songs from the Treorchy Male Voice Choir with whom I had had a long association.

As for Tongwynlais, when I was asked after my retirement to speak at the opening of the Lewis Arms I was able to boast about the village I had known a long time, because it had everything I could wish for. It had three pubs, at the time, it had cafés, shops – that seemed never to shut, whatever the weather – and it had a nice atmosphere about it. An ideal environment in which to bring up children. It changed quietly over the years because of the increase of the population, with various estates being built towards the north, towards the east. And of course the A470 didn't exist when we first moved in, so lots of changes have occurred over the years.

The Lewis Arms was always part of my week when I was home for all those years. It was renovated recently with beautiful decoration inside, the colourful outside is attractive and they've maintained its huge red dragon, which is a symbol to everybody who passes that you're entering special Welsh territory. So after three years in the RAF and 60 years at the BBC, here I am now enjoying my old age, in Tongwynlais with old friends whom I still meet from time to time. I cannot deny that there are difficult days in retirement with ill health and empty days, after sixty years of frenetic activity with the BBC, but the important thing now is that I can buy my *South Wales Echo* up the road, pop in the pub and generally enjoy my declining years.

In spite of my narcolepsy!

Glory days—Gareth Edwards, Dewi and Phil Bennett on the 1968 Lions tour.

ROY LEWIS

LIFE IN KENNARD STREET, Ton Pentre was rich in incident. Weddings and funerals brought the women out on the doorsteps, there was the flighty housewife who waved her older, hunchbacked husband off to work in the Co-op each morning before immediately entertaining a younger lover, and the Land Girl who returned home on leave with her face bruised from a sexual assault. Not to mention the neighbour who was addicted to stealing ladies' knickers (preferably large) from outdoor washing lines. There was even a husband-wife killing: she got off because "He ran onto the knife" during a quarrel.

Though my father Harold was born close by in Albion Street, generations of his forebears, agricultural labourers and smallholders, hailed from the hills above Newtown, in Powys. My grandfather Charlie had joined the diaspora from Powys to the Rhondda seeking work in the coal mines opened up by David Davies of Llandinam. He wasn't alone: in Ton Pentre itself there were numerous families whose roots lay in Powys and who intermarried in the Rhondda. The Hughes, Vaughan, Bumford, Lloyd and Lewis families, all from the Newtown area, intermarried in the Rhondda. Charlie himself married Louisa Hughes from Kerry. In my generation Enid Vaughan married Mansel Lloyd as further examples: both their families came from near Newtown. Indeed, Mansel's forebears in the Victorian period were working the smallholding next to my great grandfather's on Cefn Mawr.

Harold Lewis found his bride outside this circle of family

acquaintances: he married an Irish Catholic called Ellen Power. Her parents had come to Wales in the 1890s, emigrating from Waterford and Kilkenny but she herself was born in Treharne Street, Pentre in 1901.

The 1930s.

I arrived in January 1933 at 1, Kennard Street. I had been preceded by Eileen, in 1924. We lived in the end of terrace house which had been acquired by Charlie on a 99 year lease: most of other houses in the street were merely rented from the Crawshay Bailey estate. Charlie had also rented 2 acres of allotments directly beside the house where he carried on the skills he had learned as a young labourer with his smallholder father at Cefn Mawr: he kept pigs, chickens, a large vegetable garden and a couple of ponies—presumably to manure the land he worked. This was spare time activity, of course: his main employment was as a roadman underground.

My father followed in his footsteps. Born in 1902 he left school to go down the pit at 12 years of age and was working as a roadman alongside his father when Charlie died in 1934. Thereafter, while Harold kept most of the allotment acreage he gradually dispensed with the piggery, created a trout pond (the trout were gathered by fishing friends from the feeder dam near the Bwyllfa pit head) but eventually gave up half of the land, frowned over by the slag heap of the pit, to other pony owners.

My earliest recollection of the allotments included my father tickling trout from the pond on a summer afternoon (he always threw them back) raising chickens and me wandering to look at the mysterious farm implements kept in a shed behind the piggery, including a massive granite sharpening stone. I also recall my cousin Tom Power opening the incubator, allowing the chicks to escape and strangling half of them while clumsily returning them to the incubator. A photograph of 1936 shows me wearing my Uncle Sam's Welsh cap (under 15 soccer) and cavorting in the allotment: I am carrying the football rather than kicking it, almost as a prediction of my own, later preference for rugby.

The house itself boasted four bedrooms, a spacious kitchen in which we mainly lived, a middle room, and a front room (the "parlour") used only on special occasions and equipped with the best furniture. We lived, ate and cooked in the kitchen: the iron fire grate, regularly black-leaded by my mother, boasted two trivets on which heavy, black iron kettles could be swung over the fire itself, a water boiler and an oven where meat was cooked. Toast was made by holding a toasting fork to the glowing coals behind the bars. The grate provided the main heating: the bedrooms boasted fire grates but they were rarely used—not even in the depth of winter.

Illumination came from gas lamps, a situation not resolved until 1941 when my father installed electricity –though only in part of the house: Uncle Sam and his family in the middle room were still using gas mantles until the mid-forties. In the street outside the house there was a street gas lamp, lit by way of a long pole every evening at dusk: it provided free light in the front upstairs bedrooms.

The house had no bathroom: the toilet was built into the side of the house and accessed through the yard: it had no lighting so it was necessary to take a candle if visiting after dark. Toilet paper was provided by shredded sheets of *The Sporting Chronicle* or the more conveniently sized *Racing Handbook*. Baths were enjoyed only once a week indoors. They were undertaken in a zinc tub in front of the fire. My father bathed every day: there were no pit head baths so he would come off a night shift and light the fire, heat water in black-furred iron kettles and bathe in the tub, first his upper body, then stripped off to stand in the tub for his lower half. I can still recall the puzzled childlike resentment I felt when I was banned from the kitchen when my mother or sister took a bath, whereas my father and I were given no such privacy.

My grandfather had built a tin-roofed lean-to at the back of the house where he had installed a brick-built washing tub. In this wash-house the central iron boiler was heated by a fire grate below, and my mother used a poss stick to dunk the washing (always on a Monday) before running it through the hand-cranked mangle (dangerous for inquisitive childish fingers). But my earliest memory is of lying half asleep in bed as my father went out for the night shift: I could hear his boots ringing on the pavement and the sound of clattering door knockers: since we were the first house in the street he acted as a "tommy-knocker", rousing the "butties" who were working the same shift. Together they would then march along the street to Ton Pit.

My mother shopped every day in Ton Co-op for necessary provisions (and placed a surreptitious bet on the horses). There were two fish and chip shops in Church Street: one of them served faggots and peas on Tuesday nights as a change. We had a choice of two barbers, three "bracchi" shops (an Italian family called Bracchi had opened coffee and ice-cream shops in the late 1890s- so though the cafés were owned by such as the Forgiones they were still called bracchi shops).Our diet was supplemented by a regular supply of eggs from the chickens, and plenty of fresh vegetables from the allotment, with red currants and black currents in the summer, along with strawberries, and blackberries from the hedge. So our diet was basic but good: my father worked the allotment when he came off shift underground—it was like an escape into the fresh air for him. We usually had beef on a Sunday (cooked on Saturday night), bubble and squeak on Monday (washing day), and chicken only at Christmas. My father would select one of the non egg-laying hens, cut its throat, hang it in the yard to drain the blood and then my mother, sister and I would pluck it, using the zinc tub to catch the feathers. It was a job I hated.

The house was infested with cockroaches ("blackpats" as my mother called them). On Saturday nights, after a visit to the Maindy Conservative Club my father would bring home a bottle of beer, empty it into a bowl and leave it in the pantry overnight. In the morning it would be full of dead or drunkenly happy roaches. They were not finally eradicated until 1950, when my father removed the old black-leaded grate and installed a "modern" fireplace. The main nest of roaches was behind the brickwork: as my father removed the bricks my mother pumped DDT over the black scurrying figures. Already suffering from pneumoconiosis my father was lucky to survive the poisonous cloud enveloping him as he worked on his knees.

Around about the same time my father removed the "pantry", which held a cool stone slab, the nearest thing to a refrigerator (unknown at that time in our household) and converted the lean-to at the back into a makeshift kitchen with a gas stove: thereafter there was no more cooking over the kitchen fire grate.

My father was a regular reader: he favoured Rudyard Kipling's romances and Zane Grey Westerns and he enjoyed the *News Chronicle* and on Sundays the *News of the World.* There were always books in the house, kept in a Welsh dresser in the kitchen.

Holidays

Although only a pit labourer, my father managed to take us on several family summer holidays: in 1937 it was a week at Teignmouth, reached by train via Cardiff, and in 1938 we shared a bell tent at Llantwit Major with neighbour Ginnie Griffiths and her two sons Dewi and Billy. When we went for occasional day visits to the seaside at Porthcawl or Barry Island we always brought back a bucket of sand: my mother used it when she scrubbed the front step at the house and the section of pavement that fronted it.

At Christmas my father entertained several neighbours to parties which included darts matches in the kitchen and snooker contests (he had installed a billiard table in the large back bedroom), one of which famously went on till dawn next day. He was proud of the radio he had bought, with a built in record player, and this provided the only entertainment on winter evenings. The last party was held in 1939: my uncle Sam had come to live with us, taking over the middle room with his new wife Gwyneth (he had developed multiple sclerosis) and on that occasion, as a six year old, I got inebriated with my cousin Tom Power under the table in the middle room. The tipple was my father's home-made elderberry wine, contained in stone jars.

My father was not personally ambitious: he refused promotion in the pit to overman because he "did not want to lose his friends". But he was fiercely ambitious for my sister Eileen and me, and gave us every encouragement to do well at school. Eileen rewarded him by getting a scholarship to Porth County School in 1935. This was at a time when Harold was unemployed, many of the coal mines having closed down in the recession. He was unemployed again when it was my time to go to university: by then he had been discharged because of pneumoconiosis. Yet somehow, he managed to send me to Bristol University in my sister's footsteps.

The Forties

Sheep seemed to regard themselves as the lords of the valley in those days: they broke into allotments and ravaged vegetable plots, wandered the streets and proved a hazard to the scanty traffic, and at night a little boy hurrying home in the blackout could hear sheep coughing in the back lanes where they had settled for the night. Unnerving after a showing of *Frankenstein* or *Dracula*: echoes of Lon Chaney and Bela Lugosi with his murmured *"Children of the niiight…"* I remember them also congregating outside the library in Pentre where Gwyn Evans's girl friend Beti worked, as though they were longing to take out a library book. *How to Train a Sheepdog*, maybe.

In 1939 we were on holiday in Llantwit Major again, with me recovering from German measles, when my father decided to go back to the Rhondda because of the "Crisis", the scare over German militancy. All I was aware of was that it was somehow connected shamefully to my outbreak of German measles.

Still unemployed the next year, after a brief stint working at a building site in Aylesbury, my father received his call-up papers, on the same day as the Rhondda pits opened again. He promptly applied for work underground (which was a reserved occupation) so was never called upon to serve in the armed forces.

In 1937 I was sent to the infants school in Gelli; in 1940 I was 7 years old and at Ton Boys School. I still recall the rubbery smell of the gasmasks we were forced to use during daily drills, and the wail of the sirens signifying a possible air attack. The children were hastily sent out of school on such occasions, to be dispersed, staying in neighbouring houses. I was sent to Keith Griffiths' house in Maindy Road, where we read comic papers or played board games until the "All Clear" signal sounded. I always returned to school with dragging feet on such days. It was then I fell in love with a doctor's daughter who lived in a big house near the police station in Maindy Road: she was called Diana, but when the family moved she was lost to me forever. A great loss for an 8 year old!

Although Cwmparc was bombed in the 40s the only near miss we suffered in Kennard Street was an exploding land mine near Gelli Colliery, which blew in our side windows, plastered though they were with brown sticky tape to prevent flying glass splinters. Otherwise, I was only vaguely aware of world events. There were still numerous air raid warnings at night: they resulted in my being tucked in a rocking chair under the stairs with my sister under the kitchen table. I still recall the sight of her on one occasion, giggling, with her backside sticking out from under the table and a toasting fork impaled into half-scorched toast in her hand.

There were regular visitors to the house: there was George Vaughan, a friend of my grandfather's also from Newtown, with his Sealyham terrier which scared the daylights out of me. George used to soothe me with his personal rendition of *The Wreck of the Hesperus*. My father's response was to buy me a mongrel which we called Prince: he had a long life, leaving us only in 1954. Members of the Hughes family often called, as did Tom Bumford and we often visited my deceased grandmother's younger sister in Co-operative Street: she was known as Aunt Lil (her fame rested in her skills at making mince pies at Christmas, drawing chickens' innards, and laying out the dead (when required)). Bryn and Ginnie Griffiths often called in from across the road, as did cousin Tom Thomas and his wife Dolly, and the woman with whom they lived (in 'partments' as my mother would sniff loftily), Mary Cousins. She was married to an ostler at Ton Pit: somewhat taciturn he always projected an oddly sweet odour of manure but she was probably my mother's closest friend. And of course there was my uncle Sam who was bedridden in the middle room, paralysed from the waist down, with his wife Gwyneth and their daughter Wendy, born in 1940. On sunny days he would be parked in a wheelchair across the road where neighbours would congregate for a chat with him. Like other sufferers of multiple sclerosis he was always cheerful, and amusing to be with.

On Saturday afternoons we tended to visit my Irish grandmother Mary Power in Treharne Street in Pentre, living close, as she often reminded us, to Jimmie Murphy, who later in his career managed Manchester United after the Munich air disaster. She was an apple-cheeked, tiny woman with a strong Irish brogue: my grandfather Peter Power had by then retired from the pits and was almost senile, talking endlessly of an Irish racing dog called Mick the Miller. My mother's brothers Jim, John, and Tom also worked in the pit. Tom Power tended to work three shifts per week only, after which he repaired to the bar of the Alexandra Hotel opposite. Two other brothers started in the pit but then obtained other jobs: Peter to work in the Co-op, Will to marry a lady who ran a small general store in Tonypandy. Will would call in occasionally when selling carpets in the valley (an enterprise which failed—and probably was the reason for his surprising suicide) and Tom tended to turn up, somewhat inebriated on a Saturday night. He was my mother's favourite, but my father held him in little regard, reckoning him as workshy.

The outbreak of war saw strangers arriving among us: evacuees sent from Cardiff to avoid possible air-raids were located with families who had room in their houses. One was Leslie Palk, who was boarded in Wyndham Street. I knew him only briefly, but in 1990 I came across his name in the newspapers: his daughter Geraldine had been murdered in Cardiff. I also befriended a lad of mixed West Indian heritage—we knew him only as "Boyo". I met him again in 1951—he was playing for Cathays High School—we were opposing rugby captains. He later went to Cardiff University, and was a school friend of Howard Merrick—who married Ceridwen Thomas. Links discovered only after 50 years!

Later in the forties there were other, more exotic visitors, notably when American soldiers started appearing in the Rhondda. One, a Captain Vincent J Klein, had taken a shine to my sister Eileen. On one occasion he hitched a flight from his Europe posting to stay with us for a weekend. What he must have thought of a chamber pot under the bed, a washstand jug for ablutions with cold water, and an open fire to cook over I never learned—but he gave me a wristwatch and chewing gum and Hershey Bars so I fervently hoped that he would become one of the family. He never did, being supplanted by another Army captain after the war was over when my sister was persuaded to go to the States to marry Captain Frank Maddison Hansen. She remained there for the rest of her life, albeit making visits to the Rhondda every three years or so, while raising five children. My mother continued sanding the front step and polishing the brass knocker. She disapproved of Eileen's adopting the Mormon faith and never told my Catholic grandmother Mary Power.

Entertainment
Void of traffic the street was available as a playground: we

played *Kick The Tin* and *Cattie and Doggy*, and flew paper aeroplanes, elaborately folded from two sheets of paper. They had the unfortunate tendency to fly high in a light breeze and lodge in rooftop guttering, beyond reach. Shortly before Christmas a carousel would arrive, with its scattering of rather tawdry stalls, to set up on The Patch—an area of waste ground behind Clarence Street, at the foot of the hill, where the Gelli Brewery had earlier been located. A week later, the Travelling family would uproot their fair equipment and take it to another location, Treorchy or Tonypandy. The Patch was also used to play football—street against street.

During the early forties holidays to the beach were not possible, but as the threat of Nazi invasion retreated there was a resumption of the trips organised by the Working Men's Institute in Ton. Miners made regular contributions during the year to create a fund for this "free" trip. Three or more double-decker buses would be hired to collect families from the streets and they would form a procession to drive the 30 miles to Porthcawl or Barry Island. On arrival everyone would go to the beach and deck chairs would be arranged in huge semi-circles for the women, where they sat gossiping while the men played on the sands with the children. Cricket was not an easy game to play on soft sand.

These days formed a strict pattern. After the late morning games, at midday the men would drift off to the pub while the women and children were left to their own devices. At about 2 pm the men would return for a lunch of sandwiches brought by their wives, and lounge there until about 4 pm when there was a desultory wandering to search for whatever entertainments were offered on the promenade. These were few so often it was merely a stroll along the front. Tea, or stronger drink, could be obtained however, and then at 6 pm the buses returned, we all piled aboard for the voyage home.

The Workmens' Hall offered other treats of course: every Christmas there was a special "free" show in the Institute cinema (known to us as "The Works"). It consisted of cartoons and "serial" episodes such as *"Flash Gordon"* at the end of which we were each given an orange and a chocolate bar. There were also children's matinees every Saturday morning also: the show was a weird one. It consisted of cartoons, a serial episode (*The Clutching Hand, The Lone Ranger or Buck Rogers*) followed by whatever film was showing that night for adults. But in order to fit it into running time, the main film was usually shown with two or three reels removed—which left the children more than a little confused.

By 1941 after a brief stay in Kennard Street, Dewi Griffiths was living with his parents in the Institute and had access to the screening booth. Surreptitiously he used to trim a few lengths of exciting clips from films, splice them together and then project them for a small group of us—Keith Lewis, Leighton Brunt, Mansel Lloyd, and Brian Roberts—in a private showing in the basement. The spliced sequence made no sense of course: we'd be treated to the Fuzzy Wuzzies charging in *The Four Feathers* following a brief clip from *Beau Geste* and an exciting scene from *The Light That Failed*. But it was entertainment, of a sort.

Teenage celebrations: Brian, Roy, Ken, Leighton, & Dewi on his knees

My mother was a Catholic (somewhat lapsed) and in 1946 she made a determined attempt to make a Catholic out of me, by buying my first pair of long trousers (grey flannel) but allowing me to wear them only to church. For a few weeks, rather grumpily, I cycled on the bike my sister had bought me to Treorchy but hated sitting in Sunday school learning the catechism with children half my age. I had had a brief brush with Catholicism earlier, when spending a week with my Irish aunt Bridget Doody in Cardiff (she kept a fish and chip shop in Canton). I could not see the point of her insisting I should go to confession, when I could think of nothing I wished to confess. My mother's determination to get me into the church at Treorchy finally crumbled, worn down by my resistance, and I was allowed to abstain—and wear the long trousers to school. It was a relief: in the second year at secondary school I was still wearing the hated short trousers, one of the last in the year to do so.

It was that same year we paid a visit to Ireland. We sailed at midnight on a cattle boat from Rosslare to Waterford where my grandmother's half-brother Patrick Walsh ran a bakery. It was a horrendously stormy night on the boat and I almost went overboard rushing for the rail with a surging stomach. A week in Waterford was followed by a week in the seaside resort of Tramore, which Eileen had to forego because she had to return to her teaching post in Gravesend. I was retching before we even left the river on our return, anticipating the voyage across the Irish Sea. But I certainly enjoyed the bread during our stay in Waterford: white loaves instead of the dark, coarse bread we had suffered during the war years.

I well recall the seemingly endless sunny days of 1944: prior to going to secondary school we ranged daily beyond the coal tips to the open space of the golf club (opened by the Prince of Wales but sadly decayed during the war years). The scarred machinery of the deserted Bwllfa Pit was available to us to play in, rusting boilers serving as submarines, and there was the towering "Seven Giants" mountain to climb. When the pit was still open coal tubs were winched down "The Incline" for loading into wagons on the sidings next to Ton Pentre Football Club. When they were winched back up to the pit, empty, it was an exciting opportunity to hitch a brief ride.

No one ever lost a limb doing so, but it was a highly dangerous practice, as was the smoking of "torchy"—the decayed rope stripped from the inside of discarded pieces of steel cable. Discarded umbrellas were also a prize: we made bows and (lethal) arrows from the steel umbrella spokes. The sharpened arrow might be small but it could be driven deep into a tree trunk. Less lethal were the whips we made from plaited bulrushes, and whistles made from withy sticks. Country skills!

The mountain was regularly used to play war games.

On the Seven Giants mountain Dewi Griffiths was always happy to play the bespectacled Japanese soldier so that when he was shot he could roll theatrically down the slopes. There were no restrictions on our wandering, no warnings about dangerous places—we ventured into dark, dripping, closed drift mines, fished in stagnant pools for newts and frogs, and even the pit shaft itself could be clambered about.

Winters were a different matter: usually too cold to play outside (and never outside on a Sunday, when the entertainment was restricted to reading *The Wizard, The Adventure*, and *The Hotspur*). In 1947 there was the great freeze, where the snow was piled up to three feet high in the street and schools were closed for days. Neighbour Alan Lawrence and I tried building an igloo with frozen chunks of snow, but were defeated by the technicalities involved.

I can't say that I was too aware of the shortages faced by the Labour Government: in any case, since my father was employed in the pit he received regular loads of "free" coal. It was piled up outside the coal shed hatch in the back garden wall, where I used to assist my father in storing it in the shed.

A hateful job which I tried regularly to escape.

School Years

At Ton Boys School we sat in regimented lines, chanted our tables, played cricket and football on the asphalt yard and were tested every Friday morning in English and Arithmetic. Those who passed both exams were allowed to sit in the two lines of tables on the left and allowed to read a selected school library book. I loved to read these books but rarely had the opportunity: usually failing at Arithmetic. I was then forced to repeat the tests among other failures, and fume as other boys would show their boredom at the prospect of reading a library book while I longed to get my hands on one.

Both the public library in Pentre and the library in the Mining Institute were available to me: books by G.A.Henty's and Captain Marryat, Percy F Westerman's *The Disappearing Dhow*, Rudyard Kipling's *Jungle Book, King Solomon's Mines* and *She* were read several times, as was Zane Grey's *Riders of the Purple Sage* and other Westerns. Rice Burroughs' *Tarzan* books were also favourites. My reading used occasionally to irritate my mother: "You've always got your nose in a book." My father never complained about it and my sister encouraged the habit

At school, lunch breaks in the yard could be enjoyed by playing cricket and football in our boots, which my father regularly soled on his own last, hammering metal "segs" into the leather soles. Great for sliding on when they were worn down, but horribly clanking when they were new. There were occasional "biology" outings to the Maindy and sometimes a summer afternoon allowed us to be taught outside in the yard but they were rare events. I made friends with Keith Griffiths, Alan Lawrence and Alwyn Griffiths but each faded from my circle after 1945.

Along with Cedric Goodwin (who *might* have been distantly related to me) Keith and Alwyn both took part in the Christmas pantomime presented by the Bethesda Chapel Band of Hope. I resented not being given a singing role, but rather enjoyed playing the villain *Raj the Rakshasha*. I had joined the chapel not from religious conviction but to socialise with other boys—and girls like Mary Morris and Pat Jones. It meant one evening a week listening to a sermon from the Reverend Alban Davies, a flowing-white-haired preacher of the Old Testament school and then games or other entertainments. On one occasion I recall in a sort of stunned incomprehension listening to Leighton Brunt presenting for our edification a record of classical music, enthusiastically waving his arms about as though conducting the orchestra.

I approached the 11+ examination in 1944 with trepidation: I was very weak at Arithmetic, even though my father arranged for extra tuition for me with my maths teacher, the sadistically unpleasant Mr Griffiths. He had a son at the school with whom I was friendly but though we both went to Bristol University later, where Brian read medicine, the friendship did not really survive junior school, when he attended Porth County and we rarely met in Bristol. He ended up practising medicine back in the Rhondda, treating my father in his last illness.

At the 11+ I scraped through for grammar school entry (listed as 129th in the Rhondda) and was offered a place at Pentre

Secondary Grammar School. This was a disappointment to my father who had hoped I would emulate my sister Eileen and obtain a scholarship to Porth County. At Pentre I was assigned to the "1 A" form, demoted to "B" in the second term, then after a stern talking to from my father managed to get back into the "A" stream next term where I remained for the rest of my school days. I never managed to get higher than 8th in my class: Josie Morris always came top in every subject, Alan Oliver was excellent at Maths as was Tudor Edwards, while Mary Pugh and I were level pegging in English and Latin.

The friendships I had enjoyed during my time at Ton Boys School faded, with the exception of Dewi Griffiths: he had left Kennard Street in 1941 when his father Bryn obtained the post of librarian/caretaker at the Ton Pentre Workmen's Hall, the "Works", a miner-supported building which included a cinema/theatre, billiards room, reading room (with sawdust-filled spittoons), and various games rooms for chess and draughts. I used the library there extensively. The Institute was an environment which allowed Dewi to develop his talents as a showman.

He had early demonstrated this talent by hauling me around the streets one Christmas singing carols to the accompaniment of a punched tinplate device which, hand-cranked, would emit screeching sounds. In later years he would scrape on a one stringed violin (while wearing a Russian fur hat) in Dom's, the café in Treorchy frequented by many young boys and girls. It led finally to a brief career (after winning a Go As You Please competition) as *The Welsh Danny Kaye*, miming to the movie star's records on various stages around the valleys, before he joined the RAF on national service..

The major forms of entertainment available in those days were the radio and the cinema. My earliest recollection of a radio programme was a children's one: it involved a boy and his dog—*Rusty and Dusty Brown*. Later, when the war began we used to tune in to *ITMA* and *Monday Night at Eight*. On Saturdays my father listened avidly to the football results hoping for a Pools win: he never succeeded.

The cinema provided us with dashing films such as *Beau Geste, The Mark of Zorro, The Four Feathers* as well as, on each occasion a cartoon, a newsreel, a "B" film such one of the *Charlie Chan* series, and on Saturday morning there was, additionally a serial such as *Flash Gordon, The Lone Ranger*, or *The Clutching Hand*. I persuaded my mother to give me the relevant few pence to visit the cinema twice a week, since the programme changed every Thursday and Monday.

At Pentre Grammar School there was a School Club for the fourth year and above. Somewhat moribund it was livened up—even resurrected—by Dewi Griffiths. It was there that I was taught to dance, by Enid Benbow and Pat Leyland, both in the year above me. It led to my attending dances twice a week thereafter along with Keith Lewis and Brian Roberts: Tuesdays at Treorchy Boys Club to recorded music and Saturdays there or at The Library in Tonypandy dancing to a live band (which sometimes included my uncle Will Power on the saxophone): foxtrot, quickstep, tango but never the cha-cha-cha, with a regular partner, Mary Parry.

Sport

These school years meant the development of new friendships and new sporting experiences. At 12 years of age I was tall for my age, and introduced to the doubtful pleasures of playing in the front row of a rugby scrum. I was soon moved to the back row, in which position I was chosen to represent Upper Rhondda Schools but as other boys suddenly shot past me in height, I was finally put out to grass among the three quarter line.

There I had a few games at centre, then took over as fly-half for the few games played by an Under 15 side led by Buck Evans. When I reached the 4th form I was finally brought into the senior school team (there was only one senior team since ours was a small school) to play at Quaker's Yard, led by Roy Wynne. The Wynne family lived in Kennard Street and I was always led to believe Roy and I were cousins, but I never really discovered a family connection: I suspect it was more or less a loose term covering families that were friendly. Or it might have been the fact that my uncle Sam's wife, Gwyneth, had been brought up by the Wynne family, along with her two sisters. All three girls left in their teens for London—where Sam and Gwyneth got together before he contracted multiple sclerosis, and came back to live with us. (Multiple family occupation was not unusual in those days). After the war, Roy's uncle Dai Wynne opened a fish and chip shop on Pentre hill—and got fined for using "pig" potatoes!

After Roy Wynne's stint as captain he was followed by Des Francis and then Ken Wilkins: both had left school when I was finally elected captain (much to the annoyance of hooker Brian Rees—though we became friends later, even playing for the same team at Stafford when he was employed as a forensic scientist in the Midlands).

Roy Wynne was selected as a wing three-quarter for Wales Secondary Schools and I watched him play against France at the Cardiff Arms Park. Oddly enough the only time I recall playing *against* him was when he appeared on the wing for Loughborough College and I was at fly half for Bristol University. That was some years later, of course: in the meantime, as well as playing for the school I turned out for Treorchy Boys' Club along with Keith Lewis, who captained the side from wing forward. It led to Keith and me representing Wales Boy's Clubs in 1948, at Neath. We were not given caps, but blazer badges embroidered "WBC". After Keith left school he also appeared in the Wales Youth XV. The rest of his playing career was spent with Treorchy.

I found it interesting that Pentre Secondary School, in spite of its small intake, provided several international players in the forties: Alun Meredith and Billy Cleaver in the senior side, Roy Wynne and later, Brian Rees in Wales Secondary Schools. Eddie Thomas was supposedly our coach in the late forties: he had played for Neath and Cardiff and taught Physics at our school after his discharge from the Navy. The first time I met him was when he was about to join the teaching staff: he had called to see my sister Eileen. They knew each other at school, went to Bristol University at the same time and remained friendly until she went to the States. I don't recall him giving us very much as a coach, however, and he always remained rather cool in his attitude towards me...even though he was my rugby hero.

Roy Wynne was also captain of cricket. Oddly enough, though he was a notable sprinter he kept wicket and so made no use of his speed on the cricket field. I enjoyed cricket, became captain in 1950, succeeding mostly as a first change medium pace bowler while Ron Collins, Gwyn Evans and Tudor Edwards provided spin and Dewi Hughes stiffened the batting. Though I was reckoned to be a reasonable batsman I never scored much more than 7 runs in inter-school games. Gwyn, of course, was later to achieve international fame at a different sport: he became Welsh Bowls champion and represented Wales at the Commonwealth Games. Tudor went on to Bristol University and eventually returned to Pentre Secondary as a teacher.

In the late forties I was playing rugby for the school, Treorchy Boys Club and Treorchy RFC, and cricket for the school and the Boys Club and Treorchy Second XI. I never got to play in the annual Old Boys match against Porth Old Boys. I was selected to appear in 1951 but Eddie Thomas brought along his friend Cliff Morgan and suggested I stand down in his favour. Cliff borrowed my boots while I sulked. He didn't clean them before returning them. But at least it was a claim to fame for me: the famous Cliff Morgan once played in my boots!

Apart from rugby and cricket I was in an active group of enthusiastic cyclists, led by Ken Wilkins. I rode alone to Porthcawl one Easter when my companions dropped out. It was an unrewarding experience: the weather was cold and damp, I ate or drank nothing (to save money) and ended up dehydrated, staggering up Barnes Hill pushing the bike and sagging over the handlebars on the downhill stretches (of which there were few). My bike had been bought for me by Eileen, from her first salary as a teacher at Gravesend. Later in the forties there was a group trip along the south coast of England staying in youth hostels, and sporting cycling gear (in my case bought from the Army & Navy Stores, corduroy shorts, tropical RAF shirt of which I was inordinately proud. The group comprised Ken Wilkins, John Evans, Brian Roberts and the much disliked Keith Noakes. He drove us all crazy by his irritating insistence on riding at the head of the group. We surreptitiously raised his saddle, or took turns in heading the group to tire him out but to his credit we never succeeded in breaking him. It did not make him popular.

Ken and I made a longer trip, on a dilapidated tandem, in 1954 after we had graduated. We rode through France until the tandem threatened to collapse on the cobbled streets at Reims, then returned to ride along the English south coast to Exeter, staying in farmer's barns whenever possible. Farmers in France proved to be more friendly than those in England: we were often invited us to sleep in the farmhouse in exchange for fractured French conversation at supper, while English farmers regularly turned us away.

I dabbled with table tennis at Treorchy Boys Club and the Institute in Ton, tennis with Ken, John Evans and John Jacobs at the Maindy Club (watched by a persistent, young Ceridwen Thomas who had her eye on Ken),and miniature golf competitions at the Treorchy putting green. There was also an occasional visit to play darts at the Bridgend Hotel with Brian, Keith and Ken. I always had trouble computing the scores, unsurprisingly in view of my mathematical inabilities.

As for pubs, by the age of 16 I was blooded: before dances (the girls always arrived first and danced with each other until the boys turned up) we would visit the *Red Lion* in Treorchy or the *Ivor Haul* in Llwynypia to sink cider or "Black and Tans" with a swagger before entering the dance hall in Treorchy or Tonypandy to pair off with our usual partners.

And there was always the Maindy—where you could take walks with young ladies after the cinema. My mother used to ask me why I took my raincoat with me on a summer evening: my sister could have told her—indeed, she explained to me the term she had used when she indulged in the practice. It was called "going grassing".

In 1951 it was Higher School Certificate time. I read English, Latin and French: my sixth form class was usually made up of 2 individuals—Mary Pugh and myself. I had intended reading English at university but was dissuaded by my sister Eileen: she suggested I read Law. I knew nothing about job prospects in that field but was accepted at Bristol without interview. Mary Pugh decided to repeat her year before applying for Reading the following year. After school I met her again only once, when I played for Bristol against Reading in 1953 and she turned up at the game and invited me to tea in her rooms.

Friends began to get married. Some like Mair Howells married a boy from her own school, Pentre Sec. Her choice was

Peter Wilson, rugby player and boxer. Her sister Eirlys followed a different trend: she married Doug Green from Porth County, as did Enid Benbow, who married Lem Evans, while Jean Cleaver wed Gwyn Lewis, and Marilyn Davies kept her surname by marrying Vernon Davies, all rugby players from Porth County. Dewi, Leighton and I found our wives from outside the valley.

The Fifties and thereafter

The fifties were a time of real change. I left for Bristol in 1951 with a battered "steamer" trunk, new jacket and flannels and my first dressing gown. That Christmas I was also presented with a leather briefcase. From that point onward, though my family was still in the Rhondda (apart from Eileen in the USA) I never really spent a great deal of time in the valley.

University

Bristol was a very middle-class, public school orientated university and I felt very much fish out of water, very conscious of my Rhondda accent and working class background. I shared a room in the first year at Wills Hall with two other law students: Ted Wills from Poole and Norman Lloyd Edwards from Aberfan. We were in the same law school but glad to separate and go different social ways after that first year. The only thing we had in common was the law course. Lloyd Edwards had attended Monmouth School: he arrived at our room in Down House and filled the double wardrobe with his clothes: Ted Wills and I shared the single wardrobe. Nellie (as we called him) was interested in the Dramatic Society; Ted Wills seemed interested in nothing beyond the law course and I of course was rugby mad. Ted later became a solicitor; as did Lloyd Edwards: he ended up as Lord Lieutenant of South Glamorgan (after RNVR and Freemasonry activity and having had the temerity to stand for Parliament as a Conservative against Jim Callaghan!).

In 1950 my mother had advised me it was unlikely the family could afford to send me to university, since my father was now unemployed. But in 1951 Harold obtained a new source of income: he had been given a job by bookmaker Ned Sprague—taking bets in the billiard room of Maindy Conservative Club. I found it ironic that he was breaking the law by taking bets illegally while I was reading Law at university. The job also involved "taking his turn" in getting arrested. Ned Sprague gave him some betting slips, a sum of money, and instructed him to walk to Ton Police Station and present himself where he would be arrested for taking bets in the street. It was something he never actually did: his activity was really confined to the Maindy Conservative Club where he was always careful never to venture outside with incriminating evidence such as betting slips: they were transported by our neighbour, Mary Cousins, who used to clean the club daily, hiding the necessary records in a capacious handbag.

I dreaded returning to Bristol at Christmas 1951 from the Rhondda, (where I met my father one evening waiting on the street corner with a bottle of whisky and a chicken, bribes supplied by Ned Sprague for the local policeman to keep his nose out of the bookkeeping business). I was initially unhappy at Bristol, taking my studies perhaps somewhat too seriously but influenced by the fear I might let the family down when they were straining financially to support me (though I did get a maintenance grant of £11 a year from the local authority). But the second term was brighter: it was rugby that saved me. After the trials the previous September I had been placed in the 5th team, disappointingly, but over the next three weeks I was promoted gradually into the First XV (in which there were several Welshmen, albeit older than me) and it gave me a social group in which I felt comfortable.

In the Easter break of 1952 I joined the team for a rugby tour of the Pyrenees, where my French proved useful since no one else in the team had any facility in the language. Ritchie Morgan, a wing forward from Llanelli was drafted in to strengthen the side. I met him thirty years later at a formal luncheon in Manchester: a deputy headmaster on the Wirral he was then High Sheriff of Lancashire and we cemented our former relationship with nostalgic memories of rugby in France. He invited me to dinner where the guest was Mr Justice Mars Jones, who entertained us with a flood of amusing Welsh anecdotes (as well as his horrific memories as prosecuting counsel in the trial of the Moors Murderers)

My second year games at Bristol were restricted by a broken ankle sustained against London Hospitals; in the third year I was elected vice captain under former Welsh Secondary Schools cap Ken Bevan. Graham Powell (Ebbw Vale) played in the centre and Tony O'Connor (Aberavon) at scrum half. Both later played for Wales; Tony also gained an Oxford Blue (a year researching an oval spheroid), and became a British Lion.

Conscious of my "status" as a law student I took to carrying a furled umbrella—until jeering youngsters cat-called me in the street! I enjoyed some of the law subjects and hated others; I obtained a very modest degree in 1954 and had already realised the difficulties of pursuing a legal career. A local solicitor in Ton Pentre could not afford an articled clerk; the Town Clerk in Cardiff offered me articles but required a non-returnable premium (which I could not afford), and the prospect of reading for the Bar was an impossible one: I had no money behind me and no legal contacts whatsoever.

While at university I undertook summer holiday jobs, at Margam as a scaffolder's labourer and at Carter's of Coleford, working for the firm that made Ribena. After I graduated I took no job during the summer because I was daily expecting call-up for National Service.

Articles in a law firm would have given me a postponement of National Service; in the event, after making the trip to France on the dilapidated tandem with Ken Wilkins I found myself hanging around helplessly in the Rhondda until October, when I was finally drafted into the Royal Artillery after I protested at the delay in call-up.

National Service.

It was, of course, for me a complete waste of time.

I was not called up until October, and after a week at the dreary holding camp at Catterick I was sent to North Wales for my "square-bashing," to endure the usual obscenity-larded, mindless brutality of basic training. My inherent incompetencies were vividly exposed: on the rifle range during those weeks of basic training at Tonfanau: I kept firing at the wrong target (the servicemen beside me obtained remarkable scores on their targets!). Nor was I much cut out for working in a team with a light anti-aircraft gun, so I was sent on a survey course (because I had a law degree!) and posted to Amesbury on Salisbury Plain where my obvious incompetence with a theodolite eventually saw me idling away in the stores and the pay office.

Interviewed for a commission at the War Office Selection Board I failed miserably: I could not take the inane practical tasks seriously. A Welsh accent did not help: the chances of obtaining a commission were one quarter less than other groups and there was a prevailing, sneering Army attitude that the natural response of a Welshman to an attack was to "withdraw into the hills". A national characteristic born of 15th century Welsh border raids for cattle!

I was the only graduate in the barracks, and I along with a lad called Pullen who was designed to go to Oxford University after demob were the only ones to fail selection. The rest were public schoolboys. They were commissioned.

I missed playing any sport that first year since I was crippled with sciatica but the following September the 2ic of the battery decided to start a rugby team from scratch. I was made captain (a mere gunner ordering lieutenants, captains and a major about on the field) and we were quite successful in that we reached the semi-finals of the Army Cup. I was also selected to play twice that year for the Royal Artillery Regiment, though never in my favoured position at fly-half..

Otherwise, life was dreary and boring with little sensible to do. Because the Army had been so slow to call me up initially I was able to argue for early release in July 1956 so I could start a teacher training course at Exeter University. That was a relief—they had just started painting trucks yellow at the camp, in preparation for the Suez fiasco.

Exeter

The year spent at the university led to a post graduate Certificate in Education but I learned little of utility. However, it gave me the opportunity to join Exeter RFC where I was immediately launched into the first XV, under captain John Stark. It was something of an up and down season for me but was my introduction to first class rugby—Leicester, Moseley, Newport, London Welsh among others—and in my eagerness to continue at Exeter RFC in 1957 I applied for a teaching post in Okehampton Secondary Modern School—teaching English and Handwork! I was appointed for two reasons: Nigel Flower, an acquaintance from the Rhondda, was on the staff and recommended me to the headmaster, and the head himself, W. Burgess, turned out to have played for Leicester and the Barbarians. When he heard I was playing for Exeter he immediately offered me the job.

I much enjoyed those three years at Exeter Chiefs: proximity to the beach and the moors, cricket against local Devon clubs, rugby games against leading clubs of the day such as Leicester and Coventry, Bristol and Bath, Ebbw Vale, London Welsh, Bridgend and Newport (where one of my international heroes, Ken Jones, showed me a clean pair of heels, rubbing home the skills that brought him caps for Wales and British Lions and a medal at the Olympics). Two of my opposing fly-halves in those years were internationals: Richard Sharp who glided effortlessly around me, and Logie Bruce Lockhart who simply ran over me. They played for England and Scotland respectively. During those seasons I came across only one Rhondda-born player—Freddie Williams from Tonypandy who played against Exeter for London Welsh. He also guested for Exeter on our Easter tour of Cornwall: I shared a room with him on tour and suffered from his peculiar, somewhat malicious sense of humour!

I would have liked to continue in what had developed into a successful Exeter lineup but after three years I was looking for a more rewarding job—and in 1959 was appointed Assistant Lecturer in Law at Cannock Chase Technical College. It was a small college, described as being in "pleasant rural surroundings" (which in reality meant three scrubby trees and a patch of lawn in the middle of the town which glowed dusky red in the evenings with exhalations from the local ironworks).

I bought my first house in Stafford (£1,700). The rugby played with Stafford was at a lower level than Exeter. Covering my last game for Exeter Chiefs EW Swanton in the *Daily Telegraph* put it *"He will be a loss to the first class game."* I kept the cutting for years! But I was indeed lost: though I was selected for Staffordshire in 1962 I never did return to first class club rugby. I tried to get back to work in Exeter but somewhat overshot, ending up as a Law Lecturer at Cornwall Technical College, and living in Penzance. A broken ankle playing for Penzance ended my career in rugby in 1963, after which I moved to Plymouth, to a house that cost me £4,000.

Professional Progression

I was dissatisfied with my meagre degree and thought I needed a professional qualification to widen my teaching abilities, so in 1960 I had started reading for a chartered company secretary qualification. At the same time I decided to read for the Bar. Since this meant dining in the Inner Temple three times per term I had to get an early morning train from Penzance to London, stay in a Russell Square hotel for the weekend and dine at the Temple on Friday, Saturday and Sunday evenings before catching the midnight train back to Penzance. The return journey took about 8 hours—getting me back in the West Country just in time for me to get to work at Redruth.

I qualified as a company secretary in 1964, before being called to the Bar in 1965, sponsored by Mr Justice Marshall who had presided in the scandalous Profumo case. I had met him only once, at Judges Lodgings in Bristol but after tea and a chat he agreed to sponsor me at the Inner Temple. He came down from the Bench at the Inner Temple to congratulate me on my call and opine I'd make a successful career at the Bar. I never met him again—and never practised Law at the Bar.

Life at Cornwall Technical College was somewhat stifling: the best qualification you could possess was to be Cornish so after two years I was looking elsewhere. I had written my first law book—*Cases for Discussion*--when I was appointed as Lecturer in Law (the first time they had appointed a qualified law teacher) at Plymouth College of Technology (later to be translated into Plymouth University). I took up golf to replace rugby but suffering the handicap of myopia I kept losing the golf balls so the game became too expensive!

My first day in our new house in Plymouth provided a surprise; Alan Ruttley turned up on the doorstep. He was born and raised in Wyndham Street and after national service attended Coleg Harlech to be employed later as a lecturer in Plymouth College of Further Education. We saw a lot of Alan and his wife Joan in the next decades, the two families even holidaying together in Spain and Scotland. Indeed, it was as a result of our stay together on the Costa Blanca in 1983 that I decided to buy a property there. I still have it, more than thirty years later.

HM Inspectorate

While I was at Cannock the college had been subjected to a full inspection by HM Inspectorate; when I arrived at Redruth that college also was inspected, and when we had a full inspection on my arrival at Plymouth I felt somewhat hounded. So when I saw an advertisement for the Inspectorate in 1966 I applied, and was astounded to be appointed after an interview in London. The average age of entry was 50; I was only 35.

However, the commission from the Privy Council duly arrived, my salary went up to £2,000 a year and in 1967 I was posted to Newcastle upon Tyne, where I was to remain as HMI for seven years. I thought I'd get a palace in the north for what I'd paid in the West Country: I was soon disillusioned, for the house in Darras Hall cost me £7,150. The job involved considerable travelling so a car (or petrol allowance) was provided. Initially, after a probation period (when I found myself inspecting primary school classes with a colleague) I was given responsibility for overseeing Business Studies courses in colleges and polytechnics in the north east. When colleague Jim Deans was taken ill I was asked to cover Yorkshire Division in addition.

One of Her Majesty's Inspectors of Further & Higher Education 1970

Visiting so many colleges meant I got to know a considerable number of people, some of whom turned up later in my life with surprising posts, like Director General of Fair Trading (Sir Gordon Borrie) and Alan Payne CMG, an early civil service acquaintance who became High Commissioner for Jamaica. My colleagues in ICSA were later puzzled as to how I came to know these exalted personalities; it was really the result of my wandering career, particularly as an HMI

Occasionally I was called upon to carry out an inspection at an Army school. I was much amused—in view of my national service experience—to find that when I entered the Officer's Mess on an inspection I entered with the honorary rank of Brigadier.

It was a good life, with little or no reporting to senior staff necessary and much travelling around the country, along with running week-long courses for lecturers in the summer months (where I used the young Gordon Borrie). The most memorable was spent in Brussels and Luxembourg where I took 30 heads of law departments to visit the European Court of Justice and the European Parliament. During that period I was chosen to act as Secretary to the Association of HM Inspectors—one of the tasks was to negotiate HMI salaries

As a teenager I had dated the vivacious Enid Benbow for a while but she always preferred the more glamorous Lem Evans—Porth County rugby player and cricketer, great table-tennis player. When I was appointed as Secretary of the Association of HMI I was surprised to get a phone call from him, twenty years since we had last met. He was about to join the Welsh Inspectorate and I was able to advise him on salary negotiations. Oddly enough, he and I followed similar career patterns: teaching, playing county rugby, then the Inspectorate. Also, like me, after a few years he went back into main stream education, in his case as Dean of the Faculty of Education at Swansea. It was in that capacity, in the 80s, he invited me to give a talk to his staff about establishing college companies—at which, according to the *Times Educational Supplement* I was an "acknowledged expert" after setting up several limited companies at Wigan College of Technology.

But the Inspectorate, indirectly, proved to offer a new opportunity. While at Plymouth I had been commissioned to write a law book for retail students: several more were commissioned and I was published by the leading law firms of the day: Sweet & Maxwell and Butterworths. There were 14 law texts in all. But on joining the Inspectorate I was informed I was not allowed to write textbooks. Accordingly, I attempted my first crime novel. The result was *A Lover Too Many*. It was followed by several novels, such as *A Distant Banner*, *A Question of Degree* and *Witness My Death* based on my early experiences in the Rhondda. It proved to be a profitable activity.

I began to write a novel every eight months, and also started up my own publishing firm, while living at Darras Hall. It was never very successful, merely producing a few student handbooks and a biography of a Victorian lawyer, but it was an interesting experience and one that was to prove valuable.

It also got me into a scrape with the Senior Chief Inspector :

when I wrote *Error of Judgment* I was reprimanded—for using an HMI as a hero! A black mark was put on my file, to cover the SCI, I was informed. Sensitive soul.

Durham and Wigan

After seven years as an HMI I resigned on hearing I was to be posted to the Home Counties. I wanted to stay in the north-east so applied for and was appointed Vice Principal at Durham Technical College. The Principal was eager to have me as his deputy but wanted to relinquish nothing by way of responsibility: I had little or nothing to do. I was so bored during this period that I enrolled for a Masters degree in Social Science in the Politics Department of Durham University: the degree was awarded in 1972, my thesis being published by the Joint Universities Council for Public Administration.

I stayed at Durham for six years, during which time the college was forced to merge with Nevilles Cross Training College. Demoted to Dean of Faculty in the merger, just two years later I was promoted (back!) to Vice Principal and two years later I was looking for my own college to run.

My qualifications were sound: law degree, Certificate in Education, Master's in Social Science, membership of ICSA and member of the Inner Temple. The law book writing helped as no doubt did my unusual pastime as a crime writer. in 1980 I was appointed as Principal at Wigan College of Technology. T

The college had begun life as one of the first mining colleges in the country in the 1830s. It had achieved international recognition: when I took up the post I received letters from overseas mining engineers, retiring but writing to express gratitude for their education in Wigan decades earlier. In the 1980s the college was much larger, running a wide range of courses including degree programmes in Law, Maths and Chemistry, It comprised 200 teaching staff and some 130 non-teaching staff. Unusually, the college did not come under the ncontrol of the local authority: I found myself responsible to the Wigan Foundation For Technical Education, a charitable trust. On arrival I did have one complaint from the Head of Engineering: he told me to my face that Wigan needed an engineer, not a lawyer, as Principal. I survived the criticism and spent ten enjoyable—and productive –years. It was a source of amusement to me (in view of my experience on national service) that my Deputy Principal had been a sergeant, and my two Assistant Principals had previously been wing commanders. The college now suffered from the politicians' desire for reform, of course: the degree courses were stripped away, in spite of their popularity with students, in order to lessen competition with the neighbouring polytechnics at Liverpool, Manchester and Preston. Inevitably, of course some of the courses we lost were relinquished by these colleges—to no benefit of the student population Wigan had previously served.

In the circumstances I saw it as my personal objective to market the college more fiercely: to this end I set up several college limited companies whose profits would go to the Foundation but whose activities would enhance the college reputation.

Principal, Wigan College of Technology

The Institute of Chartered Secretaries
While the small group of Rhondda friends went very different ways in adult life, Dewi and Mansel Lloyd spending their working lives with the BBC, Ken working in the nuclear industry, Brian Rees becoming a forensic scientist, three of us qualified as members of chartered bodies. Keith Lewis worked for the NCB and became a chartered surveyor, Gwyn Evans joined the borough council as a clerk and became a member of the Chartered Institute of Public Finance Accountants and I qualified as a member of the Chartered Institute of Company Secretaries. We each had to undertake correspondence courses for the examinations.

I became an Associate member of ICSA in 1964. After leaving HM Inspectorate several appointments came my way, such as Chairman of the Wigan Family Practitioner Committee. It was a salaried appointment for which I was interviewed in London at the department of Health, and it caused some ripples among certain Wigan Councillors—who felt they would have liked the position. I was also elected Chairman of the Association of Law Teachers (before becoming an HMI I had served on their committee and edited their Journal) and then in 1975 I was co-opted to the ICSA Education Committee, which involved regular meetings in London. In 1986 I was elected to honorary office in the Institute. This began my international travels.

The Presidency of the Institute was normally held by senior executives in business and industry (such as Chief Executive of Halifax Building Society) but in 1988 I was elected to become

International President of ICSA, the first educationalist to hold the office.

Normally a businessman elected would give as much time as he could spare to undertake the Presidency but Wigan College Governors were much aware of the prestige attached to my election and, after a few persuasive whiskies, agreed to grant me a sabbatical to undertake the job full time.

This enabled me to visit most branches—though it meant over thirty after-dinner speeches in the UK, including at Cardiff Castle—and preside at the ICSA Annual Dinner at the London Guildhall. Fortunately, this was made easier by the fact that I had a London base available: I located myself in the Presidential flat in Camden Town, which I used most of the time when I was not attending dinners at locations around the country. It proved to be a somewhat exhausting experience as far as travel was concerned: moving between Cardiff and Edinburgh, Lincoln and Manchester, Belfast, Liverpool and Dublin—in no logical order. There were many committee meetings to attend along with two invitations to Buckingham Palace and considerable international travel to overseas branches. Since I had no other job restraints it meant I was able to undertake more than the usual visits undertaken by previous Presidents: I visited Australia and New Zealand, Malaysia, Singapore, Pakistan—where I was somewhat embarrassed by Muslim ladies being unwilling to shake hands on formal occasions—and South Africa.

It also led to the honour of being invited back to the Rhondda by Gwyn Evans, who by then had risen to become Chief

Executive of the Borough Council. I was invited by him to give the after dinner speech at the mayoral inauguration in 1988.

It began amusingly. I was at Gwyn's house, waiting for the mayoral car to take us to the dinner at Penrhys. We were formally dressed in dinner jackets when the doorbell rang: it was the milkman calling for payment of Gwyn's milk delivery bill.

When Gwyn answered the door the milkman looked him up and down and remarked, "Still in your working clothes, then Gwyn?"

That's the Rhondda!

The evening itself was for me a curious experience: seated at the top table I recognised faces all around the room: Wynne Jones (whom I recalled playing on the wing for Tonypandy Secondary XV), John Jacobs and other boys I had played with at school, many whose faces I recalled but whose names I had now forgotten, and there was Stan Blight.

He came up and shook hands: the last time I had seen him was when I was seven years old: I had acted as lookout while he and his brother had broken into the semi-deserted golf club house on the mountain behind Kennard Street. The haul had included a few chocolate bars and two putters. I got a hiding from my father when he found the putter Stan had insisted I took. When I asked Stan, that evening in 1988 what he was now doing he replied he was a councillor, "And Chairman of the Housing Committee." Golf club raider to public office!

Better than Butch Cassidy.

ICSA President en route to the Palace

Writing

Of recent years, while researching the family history I learned there had been a successful novelist in the family in the thirties, a distant cousin from the Goodwin side who died in 1941 of tuberculosis. Geraint Goodwin's novel *The Heyday in the Blood* had been very successful but I had never heard of him previously, so he hadn't influenced me in my own almost obsessive desire to write. Holding down a full time job had never inhibited that desire: it had started with the school magazine, edited by Dewi and Ken. But it was not until 1957 that I achieved my first commercial success: I sold a short story to an Australian magazine for £8. Over the next few years it was followed by another 35 such adventure stories (and at least 100 rejections!). There were also three novellas, part of a war series published under a pseudonym (insisted upon by the publishers).

Full length books emerged only when I was lecturing at Plymouth: I was commissioned to write my second law book. A dozen more followed until in 1967 I became an HMI: the hierarchy at HM Inspectorate decreed such writing must cease (they reckoned I might be tempted to sell my law books to the lecturers I inspected!). This was actually a lucky break since it encouraged me to turn to fiction: my first novel, *A Lover Too Many,* was published in 1968 in the long-running Collins Crime Club series. At that time William Collins was one of the leading publishers of novels in the UK: nor was it necessary to submit to them only via a literary agent. The firm went on to publish forty-five novels under my name between 1968 and 1988.

On three occasions my books were optioned for television by BBC and ITV—but never produced. Had they appeared, I might have become famous!

The publishing world was changing, however. William Collins was purchased by the Murdoch Corporation, to become HarperCollins, and it led to a change of policy: the Crime Club series was discontinued. I was disappointed, of course but then two other publishers approached me: Allison & Busby and Constable. I reached a deal with both: Constable went on to publish 7 of my novels, while Allison & Busby produced a similar number. The rise of digital publishing and the decline of library book sales led me finally to Robert Hale. After publishing 6 novels for me they sold the firm and my fiction writing career stuttered to a halt in 2017. *Shadows of the Past* was the 68th and probably final novel of mine to be published. But who knows?

The novel writing provided other spin-offs. While Principal at Wigan I made a successful bid to the newly established Open Tech to develop a distance learning scheme: we were awarded £500,000 to produce a Business Administration programme. I gathered a writing team of 50 from the staff and ours was one of the few successful Open Tech ventures, coming in on time with a product of quality. It led to a personal profile in *The Times Educational Supplement* and the chance to take control of two other failing Open Tech projects originally awarded to other colleges. Then came a contract with the Irish Government to develop a similar programme, at a fee of £200,000. Once again I engaged my staff to develop it while I acted as editor in control. But when it was completed, the Irish educational training scene had changed and they decided not to publish it: I asked for the rights to revert to me and this was freely granted.

The next step was to sell the programme overseas: a visit to an educational exhibition in Hong Kong led to an invitation to be interviewed on Hong Kong Commercial Radio. Such was the potential student response that HKCR offered to act as my agent for the programme. It proved hugely successful, not least when I agreed a different agency later with an ICSA colleague, Horace Wong. He and I ran the programme for ten years.

South East Asia

After my sabbatical as President of ICSA I worked at Wigan for only one more year, then took early retirement. As Vice President of ICSA in 1987 I had travelled to visit branches in Sri Lanka, Singapore, Hong Kong, Kuala Lumpur and spent a month in Australia inspecting for the Institute ICSA courses in Australian colleges. The following year as President I visited Pakistan, New Zealand, Sydney, Hawaii as well as South East Asia again. My travels continued after my presidency ended when a Professional Standards Committee was established in 1989 by ICSA and I was appointed chairman. Since the committee normally met overseas, the next six years involved regular trips for meetings at various foreign bases, India, Nepal, Mauritius, New Zealand, Australia, Malaysia, Zimbabwe, South Africa, Canada—and a suggestion by an ICSA colleague, Malaysian Chinese Edward Chan, that we set up a training company for professional administrators in Kuala Lumpur: the Asian Centre for Professional Development Sdn Bhd (ACPD).

I had earlier established a training company with two friends, Business Training For Education.. Based in Leamington, it ran successfully for three years so Edward's suggestion interested me. We bought a property in Kuala Lumpur and Edward tried to persuade me to purchase another in Johor Bahru: fortunately, I declined to make the investment.

ACPD ran for six years under our twin control, but Edward got into personal financial difficulties, I withdrew from personal activity and he sadly committed suicide when his financial troubles became too burdensome. His widow accepted my shares in the business as a gift and I had no more to do with training activity in Malaysia: it had been an interesting experience during which I had crossed paths with a fair number of rip-off merchants: I made a personally financial success of the business but yet ended up being owed a considerable amount of money as well. Asian business morals and practices proved remarkably different from western values. The company is still active in Kuala Lumpur.

My direct involvement with ICSA ended in 2004; my travel to exotic locations outside Europe came to an end at that same time.

I relocated from my home in Cumbria, downsizing from the six-bedroomed 17th century farmhouse I had enjoyed living in for 24 years, to a flat in North Shields and an isolated former piggery in France. I carried on writing: I wrote a trilogy, fictionalizing the life of a Victorian lawyer, whose scandalous career had fascinated me for thirty years. There was only one more novel to come thereafter.

I have three children, all trained as lawyers. On my last visit to the Rhondda the two girls were with me—and contrived to get trapped in the toilets of the Treorchy Hotel. They persuaded me not to contact the *Rhondda Leader*: it would have made a great headline—*Two Lady Lawyers Locked in Lavatory*. Shame.

So the journey has been a somewhat tortuous one, leaving the Rhondda to live in Bristol, Exeter, Stafford, Penzance, Plymouth, Northumberland and the wilds of Cumbria, to a flat in North Shields, with intermittent periods at my houses in France and Spain (thanks to my writing income), and fifteen years of international travel. But Welsh roots are sturdy and tough: my accent is still immediately recognisable as Welsh, if I hear a Welsh accent I am immediately drawn to open a conversation, and I often look back wistfully to my childhood and youth in the Rhondda: it provided me with my love of languages (instilled by Miss Bebb at Pentre Grammar School) and the professional educational values which served me well. I only now fully appreciate the part my father played in developing me as an individual: I still suffer from some of his personal inhibitions but echo his belief in education. His early pressure (resented at the time) and the wise counsel of my sister (who advised me to read Law) gave me the push I needed (a counterbalance to my admittedly lazy personality) and his financial sacrifices gave me the opportunities that eventually came my way.

And there are Rhondda friends who remain in touch after all these years…while the rest of my numerous acquaintances now only occasionally surface, to chat about old times…

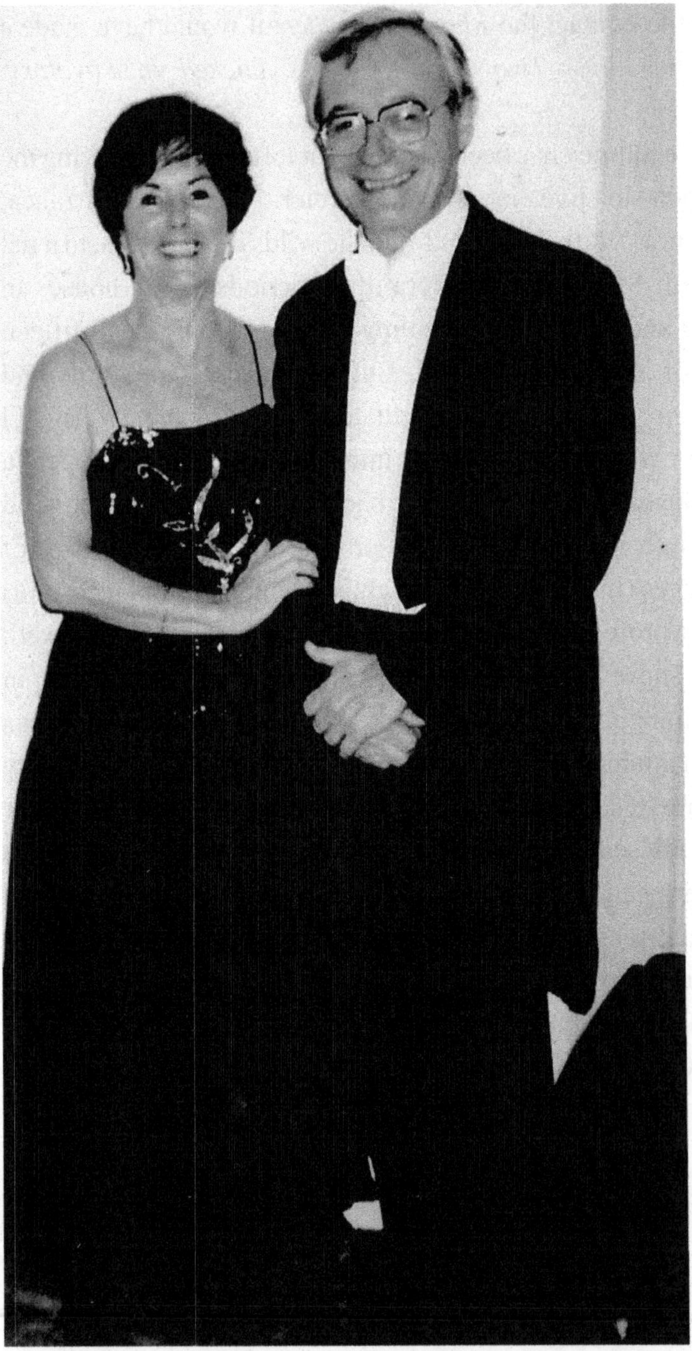

LEIGHTON BRUNT

IT WAS COMMON PRACTICE among working class families in the twenties for newly-weds to move into the home of the bride's or groom's family. My father Charlie, raised in Cwmparc, married Maggie Evans from Ton Pentre and they moved into her crowded family home, along with her two sisters Ell-Nan and Edith and brother Dai.

I was born in 5 Wyndham Street on 10th March 1931. My sister Gaynor arrived two years later and my brother, Dennis, eleven months after her. We all lived together until I left school at eighteen and started my international travel, courtesy of National Service with the South Wales Borderers in East Africa.

My paternal grandfather John had come to the Rhondda from Shropshire to work in the coal mines, had married Mary Ann Meredith from Porth, settled in Cwmparc and raised 6 children there.

My maternal grandfather came from West Wales with the same objective, had married Elizabeth and raised 7 children.

The Thirties

Home

The house in Wyndham Street was a typical three- up, three-down terraced house, a solid, dressed-stone, slate-roofed building. You entered through the front door over a white-stoned, weekly scrubbed door step, following a corridor ('the passage') leading to the stairs to three bedrooms, two at the front and one to the rear of the house. Downstairs, there was a 'front room' or 'parlour', fully furnished but rarely used, reserved for visits by our 'minister' – the Rev T. Alban Davies, for dead family members to be laid out before a funeral, and once as a bedroom for me with I was isolated with scarlet fever.

Then there was the 'middle room' and beyond that the kitchen which was used as a dining and sitting room. The middle room was only used on high days, holidays and especially Christmas when a fire was lit and the room warm enough to be comfortable.

The kitchen/dining room was the hub of the house, with a black-leaded fireplace with an oven and a hob. To the right of the fireplace a door led to the pantry where all foodstuffs were kept. The furniture consisted of a sofa, dining table (always covered with an oilcloth unless someone was coming for tea, when a table cloth was laid) a carving chair, usually reserved for Uncle Dai, two chairs, along with a rocking chair. This last was in competitive demand, next to the fire so the warmest spot in the house. One window provided the only source of daylight in the kitchen – and to the left of that, was a very large brown earthenware sink, 'the bosh' and a cold water tap. The back door led out on to a 'baili' about 8ft by 8 ft flanked by the wall of the house next door, on which a tin bath was hung. Children bathed on a Friday night. How the adults managed was never discussed.

The kitchen was the hub of the house, the fire its most important factor. Without it, nothing worked. The ritual of loading an empty grate with paper, 'sticks' and coal is a short time was worth the wait of seeing a fire 'catch' (often using a sheet of newspaper to "draw" the fire) and give warmth and light to a room. 'Banking' the fire before going out with small coal with water poured over it and later to return and break the resultant crust with a poker and see it crack open and red, blue and yellow flames come through like Spring flowers was always a delight and toast has never tasted quiet as good as that made with thick slices of bread, fixed on a toasting fork, held near the bars of a coal fire.

This was done six days a week. On Saturday I did double the amount because we did not 'work' on Sunday, no washing was hung out and all vegetables for Sunday lunch were prepared on Saturday evening. Sunday was reserved for chapel.

The houses were built in cramped terraces but they also provided a splendid view across the valley. There was no indoor toilet: if you left the door of the outside toilet open you could still enjoy the view of the valley. There was no form of lighting in the lavatory, of course but during the winter a miner's lamp was hung from the cistern, to stop it from freezing. As for toilet paper, that consisted of pages from the *Radio Times* suitably shredded and hung from a hook on the wall. The first toilet rolls I recall resembled poor quality tracing paper. It was only well after the war that there was a choice for the more discerning. I recall a conversation in Gelli Co-op between my mother and one of the shop assistants, when she asked for 2 toilet rolls. The assistant replied, "Certainly. Ordinary or non-skid?"

The 'back garden', rarely cultivated, was bordered by stone walls to the left and right on to neighbours' gardens. A the far end of the garden was the coal shed and the back door which led onto the lane ("the *gwli*"), which was primarily used for deliveries of coal.

Wyndham Street led off a steep hill (Belgrave Street) which continued upward to Kennard Street. Above Kennard Street were 'double decker' tips from the Bwllfa colliery, and the colliery itself. Behind that was a golf course, a stream and the steep mountain known as the 'Seven Giants'. The tips and the mountain were an important playground for all the children of the streets.

As a baby I would have been carried around in a 'shawl'. This mini, patterned blanket was cleverly wrapped around the adult's body, holding the child tight against the chest and at the same time leaving one arm free: there were no 'buggies' or carriers in those days. The prams, or more properly 'perambulators' were almost the size of present day smart cars and I never saw anyone attempt to push one of those up Belgrave Street!.

The steep hill could be avoided by passing along Gelli Road past Dr Burke's surgery and Bebb's bakery and the driveway to St David's Church, Incline Row and the single track railway leading to the Maindy Colliery. There you passed Ton Boys' Club, the waste tips from the Maindy colliery, and a stony track leading to the golf course and the mountains behind. You could reach Kennard Street and Wyndham Street from there without getting too much out of breath. This longer route was essential, for deliveries of all kinds to Kennard Street and Wyndham Street were made by a man with a horse and cart. Carts with coal, bread, milk, fruit and vegetables, ice cream (pre-war and post war) were an everyday sight. 'Mal the Milk' delivered from the Co-op; Ned the Bracchi's bell could be heard well in advance of his arrival; Gwilym the Oil brought paraffin. Occasional appearances were made by the 'cockle man' who measured out cockles and mussels by volume in pint or quart metal pots. And there were the seasonal visits of the *Shoni Weenons*-- the sun-tanned Johnny Onions men from Brittany, wearing berets and riding on bicycles with long string of large onions festooned on their handlebars.

There was in unwritten hierarchy in my family group. Nan was the matriarch and had been ever since her mother had died. I never knew whether she had ever had any paid employment. She was in charge of the household and did all the cooking.

My father and Dai were the breadwinners. My mother, who had worked as a shop assistant in Cule's Shop in Pentre before getting married, did all the washing in a tub--no washing machine – and the household chores, in addition to looking after we three children.

Edith assisted my mother but was always 'protected' by the family. Today she would be regarded as 'special needs': she could read, but not write, and 'made her mark' with an X. She was painfully shy and never did anything or went anywhere on the own. She was always cheerful and had a wicked sense of humour. She was capable of far more than she or the family were led to believe.

My mother and father slept in one of the front bedrooms. In the other front bedroom there were two beds – one across the foot of the other. Dai, my brother and I slept there. Nan and Edith shared a bed in the back bedroom.

Where my sister slept in her early years, I can't remember but after my father died, she slept with my mother until she left home to go to Furzedown Teachers' Training College in London and whenever she came home.

My father died in June 1940 aged thirty eight. At that time my mother was thirty seven, I was nine, Gaynor was seven and Dennis was six. How we managed after that still amazes me.

My mother was entitled to a meagre widow's pension so Dai was the only real breadwinner for an extended family providing for 3 sisters and 3 children. He had two accidents underground, both of which involved time in hospital and then rehabilitation at Talygarn – a Miners' Rehabilitation Centre in the Vale of Glamorgan. He had a superb tenor voice which was in great demand and was enjoyed and admired in the Clubs there were licensed to open on Sundays. A music professor, we were told years later, begged Dai to go with him when he took up a new post in America but Dai refused. He sacrificed a great deal for us.

The Weekly Routine

Monday was washing day. My mother collected clothes and bedding and loaded them into a heavy oval iron boiler. Water was added, when it was extremely heavy, and carried to the hob and fire where, with washing powder added, it was boiled. My mother then carried the boiling 'cauldron' over to the 'bosh' which was large enough to dip a small sheep and empty it, without scalding herself, pour cold water onto it and then wring it out before carrying it from the kitchen, over the baili, down thirteen steps and hang it on the washing line. Amazing.

Tuesday was ironing day. When we came home from school on Monday, damp washing was festooned all over the kitchen and Monday's supper was whatever was left over from Sunday lunch. Ironing was done with 'flat irons' heated over the fire.

The rest of the week was taken up with housework, cleaning, shopping and cooking. Friday we ate fish, though the *Annibynwr* was far removed from Catholicism. Saturday morning was the weekly trip to the cinema and bacon, tinned tomatoes and bread for lunch.

Sunday was chapel.

When my father was alive we often went up to Cwmparc to my father's parents for tea with my paternal grandparents. Grandad always looked lean and old and stern, seated in an armchair facing 'up the garden', armed with a catapult and a bag of marbles. If a cat appeared in his garden, he would fire a marble. The noise of it whooshing through the vegetables was enough for the cat to depart in great haste.

My grandmother also looked old before her time. I approached her with a degree of apprehension because, at the tea table, she would always stir her tea and quickly put the spoon on the back of my hand. I quickly learned to keep my hands out of sight as much as possible.

The visit seemed a duty rather than a pleasure. We never formed a close relationship with them or our Cwmparc cousins and after my father died, we made the visits less often and ultimately stopped altogether. They never came to Ton although they must have attended my father's funeral.

My mother never seemed to stop working. She was always cheerful - but busy. She loved having her hair combed and often in the evenings, in turns my brother, sister and I combed her grey hair while she sewed or darned or knitted. She knitted all our socks, pullovers and cardigans. I still have a tennis sweater which she made for me before I went to college. We spent hours holding skeins of wool to be wound into balls ready for knitting. She also enjoyed reading but had very little time for it. She had a ready laugh, a great sense of humour and remarkable optimism. She was a kind and gentle person, loving and caring, warm and generous.

Nan had the future all planned out. 'After her days' my mother was to look after Edith and Dai. In the event, my mother was the first to die in 1957 aged 53. I was flown home from Aden on compassionate leave, too late to see her alive but to attend a very, very emotional funeral. She was followed by Nan, Dai and finally, the one everyone was going to look after, Edith. The last of the Evans girls. It was Gaynor and my cousin Harry (my mother's nephew, son of her sister who died before we were born) who made the arrangements of these funerals with my brother Dennis. Gaynor by this time was a head teacher in London and Dennis, draughtsman and structural engineer, married and working in Cardiff. 5 Wyndham Street was left to Gaynor who immediately sold it to a neighbor in the street, although she later regretted it, wanting to return to the Rhondda after retiring.

Dennis died at his family home in Newtown Llantwit –

between Pontypridd and Llantirisant in March 2003 aged 69. Gaynor retired and stayed in London but died in Dennis's home when she was spending Christmas with Barbara, Dennis' widow, in January 2007 aged 73. Both are buried in Cefn Parc Cemetery, Pontyclun.

Leighton, Gaynor, Dennis

Chapel

There's an old story about a Welshman who was the sole castaway on a desert island. Once he had built some sort of accommodation for himself, the first thing he did was to build a chapel. The second thing he did was to build another chapel directly opposite the first. Some years later another person found himself a castaway on the same island and asked the first occupant, "Why *two* chapels?" and received the reply, "Well, I don't go to that one".

It was like that in the Rhondda: a multitude of chapels and denominations, grand buildings, most of which chiselled into the stone beside their names, *Adeiladwyd* and a date and *ailadeiladwyd* and a later date. The dates indicated when they were built, rebuilt & enlarged to accommodate the increased numbers that flocked through their doors during the religious revival.

Our family attended Bethesda – *Capel yr Annibynwyr* – chapel of the Independents (Welsh Congregationalist). To get to it three times every Sunday, we had to walk past Bethany, St David's Church, Hebron, Jerusalem, Caersalem and St John's "Parish Church". We were a God fearing community. The chapel was very much the centre of our religious and social lives. From a very young age the Brunt children attended the morning service at 10.30, Sunday school at 2 o'clock and evening service at 6 o'clock. The only time that we heard English spoken was in Sunday school, but the three of us sat "as good as gold" through morning and evening Bible readings, lengthy prayers and sermons in Welsh. We were the only ones who went three times. My mother took us in the morning, afternoon and sometimes in the evenings; Nan and Edith attended the evening service; my father rarely came; Dai never came.

The Chapel provided important social as well as spiritual support. There were prayer meetings held on one evening a week, a sewing class on another, knitting for the troops on a third, "Band of Hope" for the children and theatrical productions, plus, when we were older a very active Youth Club. Children were encouraged to take an active part in chapel life from a very early age. On one Sunday evening a month, a Holy Communion Service was held. Before the taking of communion took place, children were invited to recite a verse from the Bible. Some very young children would hesitantly make their way to the '*Sedd Fawr*', the 'big seat' where the deacons sat, directly in front of and below the pulpit.

The children sat among the deacons who tried to make them feel at ease, then one by one, they were invited by the minister to face the congregation and recite the verse they had learned.

At one morning service I had been invited by the chapel organist, Jim David to sing a solo. The family was delighted and he took me for a few rehearsals. Sadly, my father died during the week before I was due to sing, but it was decided to go ahead anyway. It was a short hymn.

On the Sunday morning I stood on my own, upstairs in the gallery in front of the huge organ and sang – looking straight ahead. When I had finished I looked down and saw people crying and thought that I had disappointed them. It took the organist and the minister to assure me that I had sung well, but that the combination of the *'bachgen bach'* – the little boy standing up there along with the trebling voice, the words and plaintive tune of the hymn and the family circumstances had affected members of the congregation. But I couldn't be persuaded to sing a solo in chapel again.

Baptisms were held at the end of morning services, but funerals always took place at the home of the deceased after which the men would walk behind the hearse and the family cortege along the road to Treorchy cemetery where final prayers were said and hymns were sung. At Easter the chapel rang with hymns and anthems as other congregations swelled our number for the annual *Gymanfa Ganu*.

At Whitsun we had the high drama of 'Big Meetings'. Sermons by famous preachers who commanded every inch of the pulpit shouting with grand gestures or whispering so quietly so that you moved forward in your pew to listen and then sudden dramatic pauses, where it looked as if they had been turned to stone, which brought about such stillness and silence that if the preacher had dropped a safety pin on the pulpit carpet, it would have sounded like the anvil chorus.

So our chapel played a huge part in our upbringing. I never knew anybody who went to church, although the lovely St David's Church with its huge grounds filled with trees and rhododendron bushes and the longest gravel drive in the valley and enclosed by a huge wall, blocked one end of Wyndham Street. There was a 'spiritualist' shed in Treorchy and there was a Roman Catholic church there too, which tended to be used be people of Irish descent.

The Sabbath Day was kept holy. Vegetables for Sunday lunch were prepared on Saturday night. I filled double the number of buckets with coal and chopped twice the usual amount of kindling wood on Saturday afternoon, never on Sunday. Washing was not seen on any clothes line in a single back garden in the street. We were not allowed to play outside on a Sunday. *All* shops were closed. All *pubs* were closed. Sunday was a very different day.

For the children, though, the highlight of the year was the Sunday School trip – a day at the seaside in Barry. We gathered outside the chapel after making sandwiches, packing bathing costumes and towels plus buckets and spades. We were going on an expedition. We boarded the buses and sang all the way to Barry as we craned to be the first to see the sea.

The morning was spent on the beach, taking over a large area. Behind us was a large number painted on the wall, this was what we should look for if we were lost. A full morning digging and building in the sand, playing ball games and running in delight in and out of the sea, jumping over the waves. Time then to dress again for lunch - my first experience of mass catering - for there were other large groups in a huge dining room, but we all had our tables reserved and we were often the only ones to stand up and sing grace before we ate.

An afternoon on the beach was followed, if we were lucky, by a visit to the fairground with all sorts of rides and 'games' like '*Roll-a-Penny*' and throwing rubber quoits around prizes, and dodgems and helter skelter and water chute and ghost train and a frightening and exciting rollercoaster. There was ice-cream and candy floss: our fair on the Patch in Gelli was nothing like this. Finally a slow traipse to the waiting buses and tired singing all the way home; *'Show me the way to go home'* and slower hymns like *'LLef'* and *'Rhys'*

Our Christmas parties were held in the large vestry attached to the chapel and our New Year's Eve party for the whole family with all sorts of games and competitions, followed by a "Watch Night Service" which spanned the Old Year and the New. .

Our minister/preacher was *'Y Parchedig* T Alban Davies (The Reverend T Alban Davies), a stocky, broad shouldered man, who had been injured in his previous life as a fireman on the railway. He had a half built-up boot on one foot and walked with a pronounced limp. He carried a walking stick, but could walk briskly and purposefully.

His only son, Gareth Alban, went to Porth County, did his National Service as a Bevin boy, working in a local colliery and lived at home before going to Oxford University. He studied Spanish, and later became professor of Spanish in Leeds University. I had to choose between studying Welsh and German in the 3rd form. I chose German much to my family's disappointment, so Gareth tutored me as O' levels approached and Welsh was included on my School Certificate, to everyone's satisfaction.

Alban was very well read. I still have never seen as many books in one house as I saw in his. He was a 'druid', a bard in the Gorsedd circle and a fervent Welshman. He really did minister to his congregation and was held in high regard in the community. He officiated most eloquently at my father's and my mother's funerals and was always interested in what we were doing. I wrote to him from Asmara and from Aden and always received interesting letters in his tiny, curly handwriting in return. He was ever present when I was growing up and pleased to see me whenever I came home. He was 'called' to another parish outside the valley on a least one occasion, but never left. Perhaps he should have because I feel that he was capable of greater things.

He officiated at my wedding despite having to be in Aberystwyth later the same day to attend the National Eisteddfod. We hired a coach to take the guests from the Rhondda over the Bwlch to Bethel Chapel, Nantymoel on a sunny Saturday morning in July. Alban may have regretted it later, because after conducting the ceremony at 9.30am and attending the wedding reception breakfast, it was, by mistake, *his* suitcase that was crammed with confetti, which must have taken some explaining later in the day when he unpacked.

Entertainment

The street was our playground apart from the tips and the mountain. We played in the street, boys and girls together. Nobody in the street owned a car so, as children, we were quite safe, playing simple games, which had their own unwritten 'seasons'. Today, most of them would be regarded as sexist and discriminatory.

For a few weeks, the girls would cover the flagstoned pavements with chalked out 'hopscotch' pitches where they spent hours hopping on one foot, and manoeuvring a stone around the various squares. Skipping with ropes could be both an individual and a group activity, accompanied by skipping rhymes. Girls also made skipping races along the street look easy – the boys tended to become tangled up in the rope.

The girls were not shy about turning handstands against a wall, dresses tucked into their knickers. Like most boys who tried, I found my legs flailing in the air, getting nowhere near the vertical.

Songs were integral: we would throw two balls one at a time, against a wall to a certain rhythm, singing instructions as you did so. Girls also demonstrated their superior manual dexterity with a piece of string, folded in half and knotted at the open end. Placed around the thumb and little finger of both hands, with rapid manoeuvring of other fingers, they could create shapes and patterns – all of which had names like "cat's cradle".

The boys of course had their own pastimes. Soccer was played in the street throughout the year. During the Winter, soccer posts were chalked on to the church wall at one end of the street, replaced by a "chalked wicket" in the Summer. And then there was Marbles. At both ends of the street there was a small area of hard packed earth. Here two forms of marbles, or "alleys" were played. And then there was "Conkers". Another seasonal game which resulted in sore knuckles and in modern times banned as too dangerous!

A very popular game for boys was "Catty & Doggie", usually played at the junction of Wyndham Street and Belgrave Street, facing down the hill, and played between two equal teams. During the depression of the twenties and thirties large crowds gathered to watch men playing the game in competition.

At one end of Wyndham Street was the church wall .of St David's Church, with its extensive grounds. At its lowest point the wall was about five feet high with perhaps a ten feet drop into the grounds. From the top of the wall we used to reach into the branches of the trees nearest the wall, or in some places actually jump into the trees and clamber to the ground to play among the trees and bushes – being very wary of the church caretaker who was always on the prowl and did not appreciate our presence. Most un-Christian we thought. Typically church!

At the other end of Wyndham Street was a steep slope into what was once a brook, but now covered over and then "The Tump" – an elevated strip of land used for allotments stretching down from Kennard Street to Wyndham Street. Beyond that was "The Incline", a single track railway running from the Bwllfa pit down to the sidings in Gelli. On the outer areas of the tips were all manner of things to play on – rusting trams, some upside down to use as dens, or for shelter in the rain; there were some trams that we could push up a gentle slope, hold them in place with wooden "Sprags" while a few of us climbed aboard and then it was "chocks away" as we cheered and waved and rode back down to the bottom.

The lower of the two-decker tips towering over Kennard Street had been levelled, as a playing surface, by miners during the Depression. It provided a really generous area for our games; the only disadvantage being that if you were playing on the wing or fielding on the boundary on the Kennard Street side and failed to take a pass or field a cricket ball, the ball quickly ran down a steep slope to the back gardens of the street. 'Play was delayed' while someone was designated to scramble down the tip – easy – and walk around and up the 'incline' on one side or around a gentler slope on the other side of Kennard Street – not so easy – in order to collect and return the ball before play could continue. Climbing back up the steep scree slope directly was almost impossible.

The upper tip had a very uneven surface, full of craters and dips and hollows – ideal for playing Cowboys and Indians and war games. There were also pieces of iron or wood or rope to be put to good use to enhance the games. It was also possible to build dens with lengths of rail and cover them with sheets of metal or branches and ferns. Beyond the upper tip, the golf course was where we passed and kicked a rugby ball, played 2 or 3-a-side. There we learned how to kick and field a ball, and tackled one another – gently.

Beyond the fairway was a stream and a quiet valley, at the foot of the steep slopes of the Seven Giants. There we used to dam the stream with stones and 'clodges' of turf and bathe in the freezing waters. The stream led to the 'feeder' for the Bwllfa pit which was also used unofficially as a swimming pool. We were told in the strongest terms that this was dangerous, so I was happy to play in the shallow moving waters upstream. During the summer holidays we spent whole days in this area. We set off after breakfast with sandwiches, drinks and instructions to "Be careful, and be home before dark".

Some of the older boys and girls pitched ridge tents and stayed there overnight. We formed circles of stones from the stream, lit fires and cooked potatoes – the outside skin becoming a jet black crust, but the inner flesh hot, soft and creamy. We climbed up the steep slopes of the Seven Giants and slid down again, at speed, on pieces of cardboard. There were ponds with frogspawn and newts, grasshoppers and dragonflies, and a wonderful sense of freedom.

Growing older brought other opportunities, youth clubs in Bethany and Bethesda chapels, 'Band of Hope' and later still, dances in Treorchy Boys' Club and 'The Library' in Tonypandy. And, of course, rugby: some Saturdays playing for the school in the morning and Treorchy Boys' Club in the afternoon. My closest group of Ton friends were based mainly on Bethesda Sunday School . They included Keith Lewis, Mansel Lloyd, John (Jack) Hodder, and the extrovert Dewi Griffiths.

Dewi lived in the Workmen's Hall, where we enjoyed the cinema. There would be 'two distinct houses' from Monday to Saturday evenings. On Saturday morning there was a children's cinema programme – *Buck Rogers, Hopalong Cassidy, The Lone Ranger and Tonto, Flash Gordon* – though how we heard any dialogue was a mystery. The enthusiasm showed itself in the form of constant noise throughout.

Everybody enjoyed 'The Penny Rush' except Fred Jones, the cinema manager. (Ironically, although the cinema was closed on Sundays, Variety took place during the later years of the war, involving girls in fishnet tights. We volunteered behind stage after Chapel).

The library was closed on Sundays, so then we had access to the reading room, dominoes room and the smoky billiards room. Strangely enough, not one of us smoked.

Other Ton-based friends featured in our local activities, like Roy Lewis, Ken Wilkins, John Evans and Brian Roberts. We also participated in grander annual events like the post Grammar School Old Boys Match dance at 'The Rink' in Porth and the Big 'outside the Valley' dance at 'Bindles' in Barry, premises sadly derelict of recent years.

Naturally there were also Porth Sec friends, based on tennis and music, such as Euan Gibby, who became a headmaster in Nottingham, Doug Hawkins who in later life was an Open University Tutor and Tony Basini who became Professor of Italian in Milan. We 'tennis four' played a few games at school, on the only tennis court, situated in the girls' playground (unknown territory to us, as indeed were the girls themselves). We mainly played in Blaenrhondda Park and went to classical music concerts together. All these long term friends met up during leave from National Service and College and University vacations until permanent employment took most of us away from the Rhondda.

The environment

Johann Sebastian Bach may well have written *'Sheep May Safely Graze'* with the Rhondda in mind. They were everywhere – wandering through the streets, along the *gwlis*, on the roads where they were a real hazard to passing traffic. They would head-butt the back garden gates or doors to try their luck in the gardens and had been known to enter front doors and wander through the passageway into the living rooms. Their greatest nuisance was their searching for food in the terraced streets closest to the mountains. They tipped over the refuse bins and searched through the boxes of rubbish left in the street for collection by the 'ashmen' or 'dustmen'

At one time, large areas of the mountain near the road were fenced off and cattle grids were laid down. There was also a pound and the top of the valley where the sheep were taken and fed, before being returned to the hillside. The sheep soon learned how to roll sideways over the cattle grids and proceed directly to the pound to be fed. The gentleman in charge of the pound was known locally as Will-Bo-Peep.

Coal

The Rhondda was synonymous with coal: the green mountain tops were dominated by 'black tips' the waste from underground. A few yards from the end of the street, coal wagons ran down 'the incline' from the Bwllfa Colliery: As we passed over Ton Bridge on the way to school, coal wagons passed below from the Maindy Colliery. We were close enough to both, to wander among the surface workers and the sawyers and blacksmiths at work. The only question we were ever asked was, "Whose boy are you, then?"

Our coal did resemble 'Black Diamonds'. It positively shone and sparkled in the sun. Miners were entitled to eight loads of coal a year at a concessionary rate which was deducted from their wages. A 'load of coal' was one ton and when that was delivered, you knew it. We were lucky in that our coal was delivered along the *gwli* at the bottom of the garden, completely blocking the land. Shifting a ton of coal, by hand, through the back door into the coal '*cwtch*' was a well drilled operation. The large lumps of coal were extracted first of all to build a solid front wall. Then buckets of coal were carried to fill in behind the wall and lastly the fine crushed remains were put into another corner for 'small coal'. Where housed had no rear entrance, the coal was dumped on the road and had to be carried right through the house in order to get to the coal shed. The cleaning up after this was a mammoth task throughout the house and in the street and pavement, particularly if it was a wet or windy day. It was dirty work and until you had actually done it, it is difficult to believe where coal dust can get and how difficult it is to remove.

It also involved using a pick to hack it into sensible sized chunks. This was a daily task because the fire in the kitchen was not just the only source of heat in the house, but also where all food was cooked and hot water obtained. A fire was lit every day throughout the year and although any number of strategies was employed to keep the fire going overnight during the Winter, we never came down to a roaring fire in the morning. It could be some time before you had your first cup of tea.

The collieries also provided the miners with kindling wood. Every Friday, workers returned home with a piece of rope over their shoulders tied to a block of wood at either end. My daily task, when I was judged to be old enough, was to 'chop sticks' with a hand axe and 'fetch the coal'.

School Days

Starting school, today, is often a problem in many areas. Places at the nearest school are not always available, siblings separated and a great deal of stress and inconvenience placed on parents. Life in Ton and Gelli at that time was simple. All children walked to the school closest to home. Gelli school was unusual in that, on the same site, there was a mixed Infant School and a Junior Girls' School. I remember drawing letter shapes, in chalk, on a small blackboard in a wooden frame and a teacher who told us that going to the cinema was sinful.

I vividly remember my first morning at Ton Junior Boys' School. We went to Ton Infants' as usual. Then the seven year old boys were lined up in twos and led out of the school, along Gelli Road, over Ton Bridge, into Maindy Road and then towards the asphalt playground of 'Ton Boys' and our new classroom. We were led by Mr Bill Griffiths who was to be our class teacher for the next four years. We were his new 'scholarship class'.

The school itself was a typical valley school, of dressed-stone and a tiled roof, and consisting of four classes, a single-form entry, with the boys in Standards 1 to 4 progressing from the years of seven to eleven and then transferring to the various Secondary Schools.

Every classroom had a large coal-fired stove which was surrounded by an iron 'fence' to prevent any accidents and, in close proximity, the teacher's desk and seat all-in-one. During the Winter milk crates were placed close by: the milk was kept in one third pint bottles and formed a staple part of our daily diet. We sat in rows facing the teacher and blackboard in double desks with lift up lids and lift up seats. (No leaning back or dragging of chairs). The only source of external light were long narrow windows about ten feet above the ground, (impossible to see out) and for ventilation, the very highest windows could be opened only by juggling ropes and pulleys. We were there to learn!

The greatest emphasis was on the '3 Rs' with particular attention paid to the 'Times Tables'. The chanting of tables by the younger classes was commonplace. Everybody knew the tune but sadly not everyone knew the words and suffered for it. Monday mornings for the first two years was the worst time of the week. After the attendance register call the dreaded "clock" was placed over the blackboard. It appeared to be made of some sort of canvas and it displayed a large circle with the numbers 1 to 12 placed randomly around the perimeter. The well-worn centre of the circle was black and had a number chalked in the centre. Mr Griffiths then pointed to a number on the circumference with his cane and called out a boy's name. The boy would then call out the number and multiply it by the number in the centre of the circle and call out the answer immediately. In response to any hesitation or wrong answer, Mr Griffiths, approached the boy who stood up, held out his hand, was caned and sat down again, usually with his hand tucked under his armpit. This was a frightening experience, made worse by the fact that it was so random so that it was impossible to anticipate when your name and which number would be called. Enlightened teaching method!

Four years with the same class teacher is not something I

would recommend for child or teacher. Under his didactic, humourless instruction, some boys blossomed, the middle group (like me) did their best to do what they were told, to the best of their ability and the others suffered. The teaching was formal, narrow and soulless. It lacked real enjoyment, excitement and humour and did not encourage curiosity. By the end of the fourth year, however, many firm friendships had been made which still last today. And the harsh system worked to the extent that most of us could read fluently; knew and could use most parts of speech; could write in well punctuated sentences and paragraphs; could 'analyse a sentence'; paraphrase a passage of text and recite a few poems from memory.

Our Maths lessons seemed to consist of questions about people who filled baths with water while neglecting to put a plug in or teams of men digging trenches while ignoring other teams behind them filling them in. Other subjects such as Scripture, History, Geography, Nature Study played a smaller role – while art, drama physical education were rarities. There was the occasional Welsh lesson – and music when a large chart was put over the blackboard showing letters in ascending order – *doh, ray me, fah, soh, lah, tee, doh.* When the teacher pointed to a note we sang it, but how we managed to pitch it correctly is a mystery.

Many years later, in the cinema, I saw Julie Andrews doing this, in a much happier and friendly frame of mind and with far more positive response from the Von Trapp children than we experienced. It was through this method that we were taught,

'*God Save the King*' and '*Hen Wlad fy Nhadau*' plus a few more Welsh, English, Irish and Scottish airs.

Early in 1940 the whole school was walked back to Gelli School to be given our individual gas masks and cardboard boxes with a looped string attached and which we were expected to carry every day. The school playground in winter could provide an icy slide, which increased in length and sheen daily as queues of boys waited their turn. The area was also used for the school sports day and the Inter School Sports in Gelli Galed Park, sprints, shuttle relays and three legged races.

The first lesson after lunch on a Friday afternoon was the quietest of the week. In 1940 we were required to wear our gasmasks for the whole period. This was a bit of a novelty for the first few minutes, but once the mask misted up inside, the novelty quickly wore off.

During our final year, we sat the 11+ Exam. The Rhondda had seven Grammar Schools in a sixteen mile area. The 'best scholars' were selected for Porth County Boys School and Porth County Girls School. The rest who 'passed' went to their nearest Grammar School in Pentre, Tonypandy, Porth or Ferndale. There was also a Technical School and a number of Secondary Modern Schools. It was possible to transfer between these. Primary School teachers tried to get as many as possible into grammar schools because parents wanted to give their girls better opportunities in life than they had and did not want their boys to go 'down the pit'.

Of our class of 30, five went to Porth County, six went to Pentre Sec and three of us to Porth Sec with more being transferred from the Secondary Modern School to Pentre Sec a year later. A total of fifteen. Fifty percent. Thank you Bill Griffiths.

Gwli, with sheep

The Forties
As the months passed in 1939, there was increasing talk of war with Germany. My parents' generation had already been through a World War and explained to us what a devastating was of life it was when people who didn't know one another were intent on killing their 'enemies' in their millions.

Our next door neighbour, Mr Farmer, who owned a cobbler's shop in Pentre, was gassed during that war. Occasionally he was overtaken by severe bouts of coughing "from the old gas". Unbelievably this did not prevent him from sitting at his last in his shop on Pentre hill, putting a handful of small nails into his mouth and then fixing soles to welts of shoes with a skilful and mesmerising rhythm, transferring nails from out the leather and hammering in – a sort of rhapsody in shoe.

Men like Mr Farmer were hoping that they wouldn't witness a second World conflict but it was not to be.

On the day that Neville Chamberlain made his announcement, I was confused. September 3rd 1939 was a lovely sunny Sunday morning. My father had taken me for a walk up the Maindy mountain. This was most unusual. Firstly, my father didn't normally walk that far and secondly, I was missing Sunday morning chapel. When we came down, the nearest streets were filled with groups of people talking. We were told that war had been declared and I couldn't understand why people were so sad. The only context in which I had heard the word, 'declared' was cricket, where the dominating side laid down a challenge to their opponents which the challengers usually won – without a shot being fired. I thought that the war was at least delayed, if not averted altogether.

At first, life went on as usual. Mining was a reserved occupation but soon we began to see the unusual sight of a man in uniform. Food was rationed but it didn't make a great deal of difference to us who were not accustomed to luxuries and more than content with a very basic diet. The nights became darker but no street lamps were lit and no lights were to be seen from any buildings. This was "the Blackout", supervised by A.R.P. wardens and great fun as far as we were concerned, as children.

At home, the '*cwtch*' under the stairs was cleared, so that we three children could sleep there during an air raid. This again was fun, or it was until a great chunk of a terraced street was destroyed by a stray bomb in Cwmparc one night in 1941, not far from where my grandparents lived, killing 26 people including three evacuees. We were in the 'shelter' that night. The houses were never rebuilt.

A bomb was also dropped on the 'Seven Giants' and we went up the see the huge crater. The biggest difference to us, as children, and to long suffering parents was the introduction of "Double British Summer Time" when daylight seemed never ending.

Two very different groups of strangers came into the valley – evacuees from Cardiff and London and American Servicemen. The second group was very popular with the local girls and quite popular with children because of their generosity with chewing gum and chocolate. We listened to the radio news broadcasts believing all that we were told when the tide had turned in our favour.

It was the war that was responsible for news readers broadcasting their names for the first time. "This is the news read by Alvar Liddell" – so that we knew who they were. Pre-war, they were anonymous and not the 'celebrities' they are today. Everything came to a standstill when Winston Churchill broadcast – but we also listened and ridiculed the German propaganda transmissions by 'Lord Haw Haw'. He was captured and hanged for treason at the end of the war. Following 'D Day' and the Allies gradually ridding more and more of Europe of the Nazis we felt that the end was in sight and the whole country was able to celebrate on VE day. Street parties were held throughout the country.

The War in the Far East remained to be won, but we certainly had no idea what a violent end it would be with the atomic bomb being used on two occasions with devastating results.

Rationing remained for years afterwards, but at least the street lights came on again.

Porth Sec

I just managed to scrape into the Grammar School. It was the school furthest from home and in a four form entry I found myself in 1D.

My first morning was memorable. In an overcrowded double-decker Rhondda Transport Company bus, I was sick. Not the most low profile of beginnings, and for a while I was the only passenger on the bus with a double seat to myself.

It felt most unnatural to be going from one specialist classroom to another, adjusting to more teachers than I had seen in my life, remembering their names and locations, and carrying an alarming number of text books and exercise books in my shiny new leather school satchel. Making new friends was easier than I had expected and tales of initiations and bullying by older pupils turned out to be untrue. The change suited me, for at the end of the first term I was promoted to 1C and in the second term to 1B. I came top again at the end of the year but spent my second year still in the B stream, until I finally made it into 3A. I must have peaked early, because I never came top again, throughout my school or college years.

I thoroughly enjoyed my years at Porth Sec – although there were no playing fields, only two playgrounds to separate boys and girls. The school was a two-storey construction, the last building on an estate of terraced houses. Classrooms were on both sides of a central corridor on the ground floor which had the science lab at the end of the corridor. Upstairs there were more classrooms, an Art Room, the 'Hall' which was used for school assemblies and doubled as a gymnasium. This also housed the Staffroom for female teachers and the Headmaster's office. The only recreational areas were two tarmac playgrounds, one for boys (overlooked by the male teachers' staffroom) and the other for girls. A high stone wall separated the playgrounds – with a double gate in the centre (never opened) though which it was possible to see the opposite sex at play. At the bottom end of the playground were blocks of lavatories.

On the right hand side of the boys' playground there were tall iron railings, overlooking a fall of 50 feet or so to the main Porth – Trealaw Road. In games periods (mainly for soccer), it was essential to keep the ball low. If it went over the railing and bounced on the road, it would land another 50 feet below in the Rhondda River, never to be seen again, or if you were lucky, it merely rolled down the main road and ended in the bus depot of the Rhondda Transport Company.

Dewi, Mansel Lloyd, John Hodder & Leighton
Treco Bay, Porthcawl

Post-war, a 'house system' was introduced and although it did not involve any inter-house games, it made for some memorable St. David's Day Eisteddfodau. For the whole of February there were lunch time competitions; prelims for musical offerings of great variety, solos, duets, choirs, instruments of all sorts hear for the first time, poetry recitations and essays, unseen translations for results to be read out on St. David's Day itself when finalists in all categories appeared on the stage. A wonderful morning's entertainment, followed by a half-day holiday, when most of us chose to ignore the school buses and walked home in happy groups.

A younger group of teachers returned after the war service, but the most influential as far as my group of school friends was concerned was a young music mistress in her first teaching post. She organised trips for us to appreciate 'live music'. There were no after-school clubs or societies (perhaps because of the War), but now there were coach trips of girls and boys going to Mountain Ash, Bridgend, Cardiff and Swansea to see, as well as hear, concerts and symphonies- -- Kathleen Ferrier in Cardiff and Ralph Vaughan-Williams conducting his London Symphony in the Brangnwyn Hall in Swansea. She formed a school choir (sadly girls only) but they competed in *Urdd Eisteddfodau* and we were there to support.

Although not one of the Grammar Schools in the Valley had a playing field, all of them fielded Rugby teams and Hockey teams. Opportunities to play came in the fifth form. There was a great exodus from school at sixteen after 'O. Levels' so that young people could start earning. In our situation, where the games master didn't know very much about the game, team selection and coaching was entrusted to the captain of rugby. It was very much a baptism of fire, for your first 'trial' was actually your first game.

I was invited to play wing forward for my debut on a rugby field and having had a few very basic instructions, I trotted out with the school XV to play an away fixture against Tonyrefail Grammar School, which *did* have its own playing field. The outside half I was told to 'mark' was Cliff Morgan. For the next three years I played outside half (occasionally at centre) for the School, then Treorchy Boys' Club and later Treorchy R.F.C.

Playing rugby included a huge bonus: a communal bath or shower after the game. It brought an end to the Friday night tin bath routine in the Winter. In the Summer I went with my Uncle Dai to the pithead baths in the Parc Colliery. Bliss.

When 'A Level' examinations began, pupils were only required to attend school on the days when they had exams. These were quite spread out, and when we had completed our papers, we left school, a slow, more low-key version of Mendelsohn's *"Farewell Symphony"*. Various friendships continued but we never met as a group again.

For the boys, who were then eighteen years of age, two years 'National Service' awaited us.

National Service

I had a short break after leaving school, and took a laboring job in Margam – a very different and exhausting existence to that of being a schoolboy. Some of my contemporaries were already in uniform but I had to wait until the Autumn. After a medical examination in Cardiff, I was told to report to Dering Lines, Brecon. It was to be the Army for me.

At Brecon I joined a group of young men, all with very little luggage, chatting nervously. We were ushered aboard a truck with slatted wooden benches on either side. The tailboard was raised and locked and, like human luggage, we were on our way to Dering Lines, our 'home' for the next fourteen weeks basic infantry training.

We passed sentries at the camp barrier to enter an unfamiliar world. At times, it even seemed like a different planet. In a blur, we were kitted out from head to toe (without a single measurement being taken), and also given equipment which we had no idea how to put together, every eventuality covered, down to our very own knife, fork and spoon. Everything was done at a frantic pace and "the last two" to complete any instructions were assigned extra tasks as the end of the day.

We were constantly hassled, harangued, harried, intimidated, shouted at, sworn at and always at pace. We slept in our barrack room 'dormitories' and were woken by loud shouts, obscenities and two dustbin lids being banged together. The greatest amount of time was spent on drill. We were taught how to march, turn, salute, mark time, quick march, slow march and "double". When we had completed the basics, we did it all again and again with rifles. This took place in all weathers and our only means of drying clothes was to place them on the fire guard around the stove in the middle of the barrack room – layer on layer steaming overnight. The evenings were devoted to cleaning belts and packs, badges and buckles, and shining boots, worn all day, to an astonishing degree. Kit inspections, where everything had to be folded and laid out perfectly on beautifully made beds – which nurses would have been proud of – usually ended with everything overturned and thrown on the floor and another inspection held an hour later. We were also competing against the new recruits in the adjoining barrack rooms. Our drill sergeant and barrack room corporal wanted us to be 'the very best'. All very demanding, exhausting and stressful.

There was also weapons training and five and ten mile marches in full kit. We were not allowed out of the barracks into Brecon for the first four weeks and only then in uniform and having been inspected by the military police at the guardroom gate. Brecon is a lovely, small market town, and the surrounding Brecon Beacons of great beauty, but in November and December not at their most attractive.

Many days were spent on the firing ranges where the strong winds had blown the targets off their frames – but we still had our scores recorded. We fired rifles, Bren guns, Sten guns and threw grenades. A wealth of new skills. Following our "passing out parade" we were sent on leave and returned to discover what next awaited us.

Most of the 'draft' was either posted to the Royal Welsh Fusiliers in Berlin or to the South Wales Borderers in Asmara, Eritrea. I had studied 'A' Level German and hoped to be posted to Germany. When I found myself on the list for Yellow Fever jabs, I asked to see one of the officers in charge of our training – but was told that, "nothing could be done". Embarkation leave was followed by a "special train" journey from Brecon to Liverpool. I was sick on the Mersey Ferry en route to the docks to board, *'The Empire Pride'*.

For the next four weeks we wondered whose Empire it was the pride of because there was sea sickness on an unbelievable scale. We were accommodated deep down in the ship where we slept in hammocks slung haphazardly over the long tables and benches (the mess decks where we ate all our meals) and where many were ill during the night. Comparisons were made with ships which transported convicts to Australia in bygone days. After days of wintry weather and high seas, things calmed down, the sun shone and we were able to enjoy fresh air on the open decks. Various groups disembarked at ports along the way until we arrived at our destination – the port of Massaura on the Red Sea. On firm ground again, we boarded a very comfortable train (the *Vittorina*) and travelled a hundred or so miles and seven and a half thousand feet high to Asmara, the capital city of Eritrea, and our new home Gaggiret Camp.

A handbook for the use of visitors was given to us, which described the country:*"With its crops insufficient for its needs, its lack of rivers and precarious rainfall, its deforested surface and dull coastline, what claims to interest can be boasted by this little triangle of Africa?"*

But why were we there?

Eritrea had been colonised by Italy in the late 1800s and the Italian Army had surrendered to the British Army in 1941. Post-war it had been administered by the British Military but during our stay was under Civilian British Administration with many of the pre-war Italian officials still in place. A United Nations Commission was deciding what the future of the country would be – and taking their time about it.

The locals wanted neither Italians, British or Ethiopians but it was a divided population of Coptic Christians, Muslims and Minor tribes – with no national language. The British Military presence was required in order to police the activities of the *Shifta* – the local term used for bandits or outlaws whose lawlessness was causing a great deal of concern in rural areas. *That* was our mission!

In Asmara we now spent our days in K.D. (Khaki Dull)

short-sleeved shirts and shorts, hose-tops worn over our usual socks, puttees (long strips of woollen khaki bandage like cloth at the end of which was a long half inch cotton strip which covered the tops of our boots and ankles (worn instead of gaiters)) and boots. We were still housed in single storey huts – but these had individual rooms either side of a central corridor with washrooms and lavatories at the end of the corridor. There were no doors or curtains to the 'rooms' but still amounted to a greater degree of privacy than hitherto. Also the contrast between the wintry conditions of the Brecon Beacons and the sunshine and pleasant climate of Asmara was most welcome. What's more we were still surrounded by mountains, which had a wild beauty of their own.

We patrolled them, escorted convoys of vehicles along the superb, winding mountain roads built by the Italians, spent nights sleeping under the stars, doing 'detachments' in places whose names I have forgotten, or never knew. We searched native villages, where long suffering adults and wide-eyed children stared as complete strangers (in every sense) armed with rifles walked slowly through their homes and out again without a word being exchanged. We experienced the dryness and thin air of the mountains and the searing heat and all enveloping humidity of Marsawa and the coast. But at Asmara life continued as before – drill, weapons training, parades and guard duty.

In H.Q. Company I trained as a signaler which also meant operating the battalion telephone exchange, twenty hour shift work. We did not play rugby at the time so I played some soccer, hockey and ran cross country for the battalion against the Royal Berkshire Regiment, also stationed in Asmara. There were also pick-up games of basketball and touch rugby – and the twice weekly practices and the concerts we gave as the battalion choir were a refreshing change from the daily military routine.

Asmara itself was an attractive, Italianate, modern town which had expanded rapidly in the thirties as the main base for Mussolini's Ethiopian War. It had European and native areas and some excellent Italian restaurants. A group of us found one which was not frequented by any other military personnel. Among our group were Ugo Carpanini whose family owned two restaurants in Cardiff and was now the battalion interpreter, and 'Chick' Fowler who hailed from Warrington and was bound for Oxford University to read Modern Languages. He already had an excellent command of the Italian language, so we were always made most welcome. Our farewell visit was quite an emotional one.

There was a NAAFI club in town in addition to the one on camp, but some of the lads took advantage of the company of the local native women. This was no great temptation for me – probably the result of a combination of a chapel upbringing and the periodic mandatory attendance at the showing of the V.D. films on camp. We always went into town in 'civvies' and appreciated the experience of life outside camp.

We were never given any leave: there was nowhere outside Asmara we would have wanted to go. There were no 'Rest Camps' or 'Leave Centres' which existed in other postings.

Nevertheless, time passed fairly quickly and during our final few months we were encouraged to sign on – to very little effect. We had had enough.

Many of us had been promised places at Teacher Training Colleges or Universities and were returned to the U.K. in good time to begin the Academic Year. It was a more comfortable journey by troopship at this time of year. The final gathering of our close group of half a dozen was at Ugo Carparni's twenty first birthday party at his family home in Cathedral Road, Cardiff. A splendid celebration before we were 'demobbed' – but still kept our uniforms, because we had three years to serve and three two-week camps to attend as Reservists.

College

The College of St. Mark and St. John in Kings Road Chelsea was to be my home for the next two years. The timing was perfect. I was in London at the time of 'The Festival of Britain' and a new adventure had begun.

Lecturers and Tutors in Colleges must have had a shock after the introduction of National Service. Instead of receiving pupils straight from school, they now were faced with young men who had been through years of real life experiences and were far more mature.

For us, student life brought a sense of freedom and opportunity: apart from Festival of Britain, there were clubs and societies to join in college, plus an abundance of Ladies' Teacher Training Colleges who invited us to dances on Saturday evenings. I studied English and Physical Education, while the whole year group attended a variety of Education lectures. We visited local schools, did 'demonstration lessons' before a small group of our peers and did three week blocks of 'teaching practice'.

Then there was rugby. We played our home games on the Civil Service ground in Chiswick and for two terms we had matches on Wednesday and Saturday afternoons. I was selected for the first fifteen in the first year and captained the college club in the second year. It was a most successful season for we lost only one game. Our opponents were other London Teacher Training colleges – one of which was St Mary's at Strawberry Hill where their outside half was Martin Regan who was playing for England at the time. We also played Police District Teams and the Joint Services School of Linguists when Carwyn James was playing while studying Russian there.

One rugby-free Saturday fellow student Geoff Whitson (who later played for Newport and Wales) suggested that we applied to London Welsh RFC to have a game in one of their five teams. We were offered a game in the second fifteen, "The Druids", where I played in the centre and kicked two drop goals. During the following week I was invited to play for the first fifteen against Neath on the following Saturday. We had an important college game, so I declined but decided to apply for a teaching post within reasonable access to London and join the club the following season.

Geoff had arranged to meet a girl he knew from Newport: she was bringing a friend with her. That's how I first met Ray Thomas from Nantymoel, who was then teaching in East Ham. We continued to meet during the Summer Term.

After the college final examinations I applied for a teaching post in Essex and was appointed to Ayloff Primary School in Hornchurch Essex. At the age of twenty- two it was time to start a career!

Professional Progression

Ayloff was a large, overcrowded primary school. My first classroom was one half of the school dining room which we had to vacate in the last morning period so that it could be prepared for lunch. The afternoon period was accompanied by the crashing sound of cutlery and crockery being washed up by dinner ladies. The other half of the dining room was the classroom of Luther Williams, a short dynamic Welshman who took me under his wing and was a great colleague to have.

The school had its own playing field so I was able to train on my own after school. I had a trial for London Welsh and played for the first team and sometimes the second team for the next two seasons. W turned out at Herne Hill on a field in the centre of the cycle track used for the 1948 Olympic Games. I did two Christmas Tours – playing Neath on Christmas Day, Llanelli on Boxing Day and Swansea two days later, and two Easter Tours when we played Aberavon on Good Friday, Newport on the following day and Pontypool on Easter Monday.

After leaving college, I had lost touch with Ray, so daily after school I went from Hornchurch to East Ham and stood outside the station watching local buses passing by. After a few weeks, almost at the point of giving up, I saw her, jumped on a bus behind and alighted at the stop where she got off. Surprise!

We started dating again. At home there was a problem: the

Bwlch Road, linking the Rhondda and Ogmore Valleys and leading to the coast in Porthcawl, had no bus service. To walk along the long winding road on both side of the mountain would have taken hours so I took the direct route and clambered straight up the mountain on the Rhondda side and scrambled down the Nantymoel side. Fortunately Ray lived in one of the streets at the top end of the valley. The timing was right too, because a few years later the forestry commission planted trees covering the mountain on the Ogmore Side. We became engaged at Christmas 1954 and were married in Nantymoel in July 1955. Ray's parents had moved house by this time, to a terraced house directly opposite that of Lyn Davies, Olympic Gold Medalist in Tokyo whose winning jump of 8.23m (27 feet) was painted in white lines on the pavement outside his parents' house.

In September 1955, a good number of pupils and staff from Ayloff moved into Durringford County Primary School just outside Hornchurch where there was a mixture of old and new staff, a young enthusiastic headmaster and a deputy headmistress is her first deputy headship. She introduced Country Dancing in school. Ray and I became enthusiasts, it was enjoyed by children in schools, at staff functions and somewhat bizarrely at some in-service training in Saudi Arabia later, during the first Gulf War.

Teaching overseas

Ray and I had decided to travel, before settling down. We looked at posts overseas in Service Children's Schools and, having already taught children from the RAF station in

Hornchurch, applied to the Air Ministry. I specifically applied for Aden because it was a two year contract whereas most others were three. I was appointed to a post in the RAF children's school in Khormaksar, Aden in September 1957. We were certainly in for new experiences far away from home.

There was a lack of married accommodation, so I had to travel unaccompanied and was put on a waiting list for accommodation. What I hadn't been told about Aden was that it had formerly been a 'punishment station' for units of the British Army because of its climate. You don't know the true meaning of humidity until you have experienced the feeling of opening a door on a beautifully sunny morning and feeling as if someone had thrown a hot, soaking blanket around you and you can't see because your spectacles or sunglasses have immediately misted up. We changed clothes three times a day in the worst weather. There was no relief in going into the sea, which felt like warm soup. When you came out, you just stood still to dry off and salt patches appeared on your skin. You didn't feel free of stickiness until you had a warm shower and then toweled yourself slowly and dressed in slow motion.

We used the 'Civilian Officers Mess', which catered for teachers, Air Ministry Civil Servants, Met Officers and SSAFA sisters. With its mixed dining facilities and a bar it provided a friendly and comfortable environment, and air-conditioned, something of a rarity when most hotels and shops had large ceiling fans.

Aden was originally a settlement of the British East India Company who occupied the territory to prevent pirates attacking shipping on its way to India. It was an important refueling port and became even more important after the opening of the Suez Canal. In 1937 it was separated from British India and became a Crown Colony of the UK. From its previous coal-bunkering days, I was pleased to see a familiar name, *Cory Brothers*, on the seafront.

RAF Children's School at Kormaksar was an all age school, primary and secondary. The classrooms were converted RAF buildings, pending the building of a new school. My first classroom was the Billiard Room of the Officers' Mess which I had to vacate for a long lunchtime daily!

We worked mornings only so afternoons were spent at Tarshyne Officers' Club at Steamer Point, or in the sea, on the tennis court or in the shade under *Bashas* on the beach (four tall corner poles covered with rush mats). A very different life style from the Rhondda!

I finally got a 'hiring', not married quarters on the base but a flat in a block which had been taken over by the military to ease the waiting list. Great news. Ray was given permission to join me and sailed from Tilbury on the P&O's *Strathmore* on 12th October.

The timing was poor. Nasser had nationalized the Suez Canal Company in late 1956 and matters were far from settled with Britain and France. The *Strathmore* had arrived in Malta when Israel invaded Egypt, and was then ordered to return to Gibraltar, to disembark all passengers bound for Egypt (who would fly back to UK) and then sail the 'old route' around the Cape.

When Ray sent a signal asking for advice my headmaster recommended that she should stay on board because, if she didn't come out now, there was no knowing when she would be given permission. Ray and other wives rushed back to the ship, sailed around the Cape, stopped briefly in Cape Town and Durban and disembarked in Bombay. They were then flown, Air India, from Bombay to Aden, arriving on 6th December.

It was a really good, very different, Christmas in the sunshine. Before school closed, Father Christmas had arrived by helicopter, ridden on a camel to the school building, met the children and distributed presents in the open air before leaving again on the same transport. And in the New Year, Ray was offered a post as a 'locally engaged teacher' so life was going to be busy.

Mess life was fun. Teachers were granted 'Officer Status' at the Officers' Club at Tarshyne on the beach at Steamer Point. This had a swimming pool in addition to being able to swim in the sea – our particular beach being enclosed by a shark net. We also attended functions at the Officers' Mess in R.A.F. Khormaksar – the Christmas ball being quite spectacular.

Though 1956 ended on a high, the New Year began with a shock. I received a call: my mother was in hospital, severely ill. I was granted compassionate leave to fly home immediately.

It was a long restless flight to the U.K. I desperately wanted to see my mother, and spend some time together. Sadly it was not to be. As soon as I arrived in England I was told she had died the previous day. It was a very emotional homecoming and the house was a most depressing place to be for the next four days while arrangements were made for the funeral. At Treorchy cemetery on a cold, wet day in driving rain a large group of people stood around the grave to hear Alban's final tribute to my mother, prayers and a heart wrenching rendering of '*O fryniau Caersalem*'.

A feature of teaching overseas was that everyone gave generously of their time, giving lifts to school, shopping trips and social functions. Neither Ray nor I could drive, but driving lessons were quickly arranged and once we received our driving licences we obtained our very first car – a brand new Volkswagen Beetle, ADX 9796, bright orange in colour and known as the 'Salmon Tin'. Why choose that colour? It chose us. It was the last one in the V.W. showroom – one of the last shipments to arrive before the Suez Canal closed.

The Civilian Mess was popular because the single female teachers drew the young officers to a more normal social life – and we enjoyed the various traditions of the military officers' messes. Also, our social circle widened considerably for three reasons – broadcasting, rugby and tennis.

Broadcasting

Army signaller on National Service

The only radio station broadcasting in English was AFBA (The Aden Forces' Broadcasting Association), amateur, and voluntary based at R.A.F Khormaksar. Ray and I applied to be 'announcers', were interviewed and given 'voice tests' and were accepted. At first this was continuity announcing between programmes before been given programmes of our own and hosting 'request programmes'. Some months later I became 'programme director', responsible for compiling the programmes to be broadcast for the entire week and producing our own *Radio Times* which was distributed to all messes and units. We had an extensive record library and via the BBC a splendid selection of 'Transcriptions' of plays and other programmes which we could incorporate into our own broadcasts, which were all 'live'. We also linked directly to the BBC for news bulletins.

The first programme I put out was called *'Piano Moods'*. I then did *'Music from the Opera and Music from the Ballet'* before becoming more adventurous and interviewing a cross section of Service men and women, doing a *'My Kind of Music'* programme. I interviewed Randolph Churchill when he visited Aden. On our final Christmas, BBC asked us to join the popular Sunday morning *'Family Favourites'* and we were linked up to join Jean Metcalf and forces families from around the world. Ray did a *'Letters from Home'* where she received an amazing amount of mail from families in the UK sending messages and requesting records for their kinsfolk in Aden. I was in charge of AFBA for our final two years: a great experience

Rugby and Tennis

I was chosen to captain the station XV, playing on hard packed sand, which meant no heavy falls after tackles and scrummaging was 'interesting' to behold. We played against the units in Steamer Point, the army regiment stationed here and against 'Little Aden' where there was a B.P. refinery and whose players hosted us in princely fashion. There were also Army v RAF, Civilian v Service games, while Royal Navy ships visiting were always grateful for a fixture and Seven-a-Side Tournaments. I also made my only appearance for 'Wales' in an England v Wales game which was organised one Christmas.

An end of season tour for an Aden combined Services tour was arranged to Nairobi. I captained the party and we stayed at RAF Eastleigh in Nairobi amidst lush greenery, colourful birds and a cooler climate. We found the 'downside' the first morning's training session. We were now 4000ft up and having flown from sea level, when we tried to run, we were gasping for breath. We played on grass again, but though it was hard packed and lovely to run on, it resulted in grazed knees and elbows. We played against RAF Eastleigh, Kenya Police and Nakuru and had a most convivial stay in Kenya which included a trip to a safari park, before the tourists arrived.

We played tennis most days, singles and doubles. There were always plenty of people keen to play and several tournaments held. Ray really flourished and won the Aden Ladies' Singles Tournament.

Our first year ended with another bonus. There was a leave centre in Mombasa – clusters of huts on Nyali beach – only a few hundred yards from the luxurious Nyali Beach Hotel, famed for its 'silver sands'. No more barren rocks. A lush green background, fresh fruit and vegetables – which didn't have to be flown in and a tremendous variety of creatures new to us. Our van stopped for a while at the main gates of the camp while a large snake was being reluctantly dragged from a ditch and beaten to death. The bird life was a joy to see and hear. The beach had rock pools which had an amazing variety of life. And we were fascinated by the 'Mombasa trains' around the camp - six inch long jet black millipedes with their bright red legs working overtime. We also took a trip to Tsavo

Game Park for a safari on a grander scale than Nairobi's.

In our second year the new school at Khormaksar was completed for Secondary aged children only, while the Juniors were to move to Chapel Hill in Steamer Point, a group of buildings converted for school use at the RAF Headquarters with a wonderful view over the harbour. Ray was now expecting our first child, so a surprise was in store for our families when we were due to return home for the summer.

I enjoyed another season as captain of the RAF Khormaksar Rugby Team and led the Aden Combined Services Team to Nairobi. We enjoyed school and the social life and applied for, and were granted a second two-year contract. But we had to vacate our flat in Maralla and go through the waiting list process again.

We sailed home on a Bibby Line ship which felt far more like a holiday cruise than our previous voyages.

It was great to see family and friends again – but 'home' felt strange without my mother and we were concerned to find that Ray's father was ill – although he tried to make light of it. Worse was to come and at the end of the holiday we decided that it would be better for Ray to stay at home for a while to help her mother. Her 'short stay on' was extended when her father's condition deteriorated but he was determined to see his first grandchild. Alison was born in Bridgend on 27th November 1958. Ray's father died on 6th January so he was able to spend a Christmas with daughter and granddaughter. Ray then joined me, sailing *'Union Castle'* this time and we were relieved and delighted to be together again – and for me to be introduced to my daughter.

We were soon allocated a 3 bedroomed detached 'married quarter' on the base at RAF Khormaskar. Without a handbook to help us, we learned what is involved in becoming parents for the first time and Alison loved being dressed in the minimum of lightweight clothing and became a real water-baby in the swimming pool and sea. We were now not as footloose and fancy-free as in previous years.

At the end of the school year there were 'indulgence passages' to Hong Kong for the summer holidays. The 'indulgence trip' meant that if there was any room on board a troop ship you could apply to fill the vacancy until the next port of call, when you had to re-apply to travel further, provided that you could pay your own return fare from wherever you disembarked

We sailed to Ceylon, had lunch at the Mount Lavinia Hotel, then sailed to Singapore where they kicked all indulgence passengers off and allowed the Singapore service families a return trip to Hong Kong. Singapore still had its old far-east charm in 1959 and wasn't the giant shopping mall that it is today. We had no problems in getting back on board either in Singapore or Ceylon and thus had a most unexpected and exciting summer holiday. But our time was running out: it was time for a change and to move, perhaps nearer to home. We applied to Air Ministry again, and were offered Cyprus!

Cyprus

I joined the staff of The Curium School in Limassol: I flew out on an RAF Charter Flight to Nicosia, where I boarded a coach to Limassol. The main road was narrow with cobbles or stones either side, sometimes occupied by heavily laden donkeys, while drivers of motor vehicles seemed to play 'chicken' with oncoming traffic to say who would stay on the road. An essential break was made at the 'Halfway House', a large, simple café, restaurant and 'comfort stop', which lived up to its name. I was expecting to see lush and verdant green in the landscape, but this was to appear only inautumn. The countryside was dry and rocky.

The search for accommodation was an interesting one. The local taxi drivers must have been in the pay of local estate agents for they would appear at the hotel after school every day and take us to look at whatever we required, for no cost!

. The Curium School was temporary accommodation with plenty of surrounding grounds for the children to play. It came as something of a shock to be working mornings and afternoons, a long day for the children who were bussed home for lunch every day. Once I had found a two bedroom bungalow Ray and Alison were soon on their way, by sea.

Limassol had quite a large service population spread among the local inhabitants, waiting for 'married quarters' on RAF Akrotiri, the military village at Berengaria, just outside Limassol, or at the headquarters at Episkopi. The social centre was the Officers Club & Tennis Courts on Berengaria village and 'Ladies Mile Beach' near the Akrotiri Base where military families had their own private beach and where water skiing and sailing were available. There were medical facilities for families in easy reach at the Limassol Clinic and we became great friends with a number of R.A.F doctors. We were also members of the Officers Club in Episkopi with access to the private pebble beach and bay. There was a great deal for us to explore throughout the island.

The timing of our three year stay was perfect. On 1st April 1955 EOKA, a Greek Cypriot guerrilla organisation who desired independence for Cyprus began sporadic attacks on British bases and British Service personnel. Following Independence they also wanted ENOSIS, union with Greece, which didn't please the large Turkish Cypriot population. This situation lasted until December 1959 when a cease fire was declared. So there was 'peace in our time' on the island and Cyprus was granted Independence in August 1960 but Britain maintained two 'Sovereign Base Areas' in Akrotiri and Dhekelia.

Whereas the Curium School had plenty of outdoor space, trees and shade, our new school, the Campbell School was on a much smaller plot in the middle of urban Limassol, with a small playground and no shade. The school was already too small so it was decided to build a second storey above the ground floor whilst the school was in session, plus holiday periods, which called for much patience, innovation and dedication.

I was appointed deputy head at the end of that second year. In spite of a constant change of staff and pupils there still was a 'family feeling' about service children and teachers being made to feel welcome and settle in quickly. Outside school, I began playing rugby again following a season's break, playing tw seasons for RAF Akrotiri and their seven a side team. By this time I also processed genuine service connections. In 1961, No 1 (Overseas) Squadron Air Training Corps was formed based on Akrotiri. Being based where we were, we had access to opportunities which were not available to the traditional squadrons. We also did annual camps in Malta and visited Tripoli. Fascinating.

Ray and I were still playing a good deal of tennis and our Wednesday evenings were spent in the hall of the Campbell School attending practice in a mixed choir of service personnel and civilians: choir practice was followed by kebabs at a petrol station in Limassol along with bottles of wine, sweet and dry.

We had moved from our initial bungalow to a larger and more modern one, next door to the Greek Cypriot owners who were pharmacists with two teenage daughters. This situation introduced us to a fascinating local tradition. We lived in the second and newer of the two bungalows which they owned. These were the dowries for their daughters. It was written into our contract that potential suitors could visit and inspect the bungalow on a Sunday morning, given notice, so that the dowry could be appraised.

Ray's mother came out to stay and so did Gaynor who brought Edith with her, who had never travelled further than Cardiff in her life and who was overwhelmed by the whole experience. We explored the mountain villages and vine-filled terraced slopes. During the harvest season, road signs were erected warning of 'Danger – Grape juice on road' as lorry loads of grapes were being transported to wineries. We stayed at the leave centre in Troodos, enjoying the snow in the winter and the cooling breezes and pine scented air in the summer as an escape from the heat and humidity of the coast. We visited the antiquities at Curium which surrounded the wonderful amphitheatre overlooking the sea, the tombs at Paphos, the ruins of the Famagusta and the 'panhandle' northern coastline at Kyrenia.

During our second year with our second child on its way we moved to a married quarter on Berengaria Village. Gaynor arrived in March 1962, at the R.A.F hospital in Akrotiri. Many service people left Cyprus for holidays in Egypt or Beirut in the course of the tour of duty, but we were more than content to stay and enjoy all that the island had to offer.

We now felt it was time to return to the U.K, to stay in Nantymoel while we sought new teaching posts.

Prep. School Years

The Times Educational Supplement had an *Independent Schools Section* where I found an interesting possibility. When I rang in response to the advertisement the headmaster (and owner) of the school, Maurice Averill, asked a few questions about my teaching experience but far more about my rugby experience. He asked me to bring certificates and references – along with a London Welsh tie. He said he would be wearing a Wasps tie!

It was to be a six day working week plus some weekend duties- but accommodation would be provided. He offered me the job, so we were able to relax and enjoy a few weeks holiday before entering the world I only knew through the eyes of Billy

Bunter, Jennings and Derbyshire.

The school term was busy, with Wednesday afternoon devoted to senior games or inter- school matches, and teaching also took place on Saturday mornings, with inter-school games on Saturday afternoons. There was small boarding element of two dozen or so boys and male staff were required to do "weekend duty" supervising the boy's prep and entertaining them on Saturday evening

Haywood House, next door, was also part of the school and boasted a 20 metre heated swimming pool, which was a real bonus for us as a family. One memorable night the Latin master, a parent and I met for a drink in the Bull Hotel. On the walk back to school we bought a dozen eggs and our conversation turned scientific. It was argued that eggs would not break if dropped into water even from a considerable height. By the time we got back to Haywood House, the theory was tested by throwing eggs over the roof into the swimming pool. The parent stood at the side of the pool to supervise the proceedings and I stood half way at the side of the house calling out instructions to and from both. As the eggs appeared over the roof missing the pool but landing all around the surrounding paved area the parent became more and more hysterical until all the eggs had been thrown. We went home eggless and the parent helpless. The following morning the school maintenance man was incandescent, raging against vandals.

A pre--prep school called Kingscote opened in January 1964 and Ray was offered one of the three positions available.

The first XV were usually taken to Oxford to see the

University v. Steele Bodgers XV prior to the 'Varsity match'. The 1st XV and 2nd XV were taken to Twickenham to see the 'Varsity match itself in December. The annual carol service was held in All Saints Church . The spring term always began on the Tuesday following the Wales v England Rugby International. A school play was produced at the end of the Spring Term. The big events of the Summer Term were the Common Entrance Examinations, the Sports Day, Prize Giving and Speech Day in July and the end of year Parent' Association Barbecue.

The next Christmas , Ray was persuaded to take Gaynor into Kingscote with her – so she was head girl at a very early age The following year Gareth was born and we moved into our own bungalow in Chalfont-St.Giles in the Summer of 1965. Were we finally settling down.

It was the fourth year of my being in the same classroom, the same age range and the same school calendar, when I realised what I felt that I was missing…the fun and spontaneity and the collegiality of teaching overseas. The staff were friendly enough, but the genuine bond which we had experienced both in and out of school was lacking. I had been given as much promotion as was possible. To seek further promotion would mean another move. We had seen very little of Europe and it was a good time to go when the children were of pre-school and primary school age. Service Children's Schools had been reorganised and were no longer controlled by three separate Services. We applied to go to Germany which I longed to visit since missing out on doing my National Service there. I obtained an appointment for September 1967.

Osnabruck

The authority responsible for the organisation of schools in Germany was the British Families' Education Service (BFES). At the beginning of a new school year, the staffing of so many schools was a major operation. A large group of us were flown out to Hamm for a week's induction course and then we were allocated to the garrisons spread throughout northern Germany (the Americans had the South) and to our individual schools. Half a dozen or so ladies, plus myself were assigned to Osnabruck, where there were four primary schools – Clive, Cromwell, Marlborough & Wellington. I was appointed to Clive School.

Osnabruck was the largest military garrison outside the UK with barracks (previously German) spread around the city and clutches of 'married quarters' also dotted about, as were the four schools. The Marlborough and Wellington female teachers were accommodated in a Teachers Mess close to Marlborough School; Cromwell and Clive female teachers were accommodated in Martinsburg Teachers' Mess – a large villa which was on the grounds of Clive School. All the teachers were in 'married quarters' – except me.

Clive School was temporary and a new school was being built in Belm about seven kilometres out of Osnabruck. The school had a very friendly, welcoming feel about it and once again social life was centred on the two teachers' messes. Osnabruck had been destroyed by bombing during the war – but you couldn't detect any signs of that in the modern shopping centre or the beautifully restored and reconstructed Altsadt. We were allocated a flat in the small village of Belm.

We were on the 5th floor of our block with superb views of the village. The lift system which was both entertaining and frustrating: when the lift was summoned it would go to the higher floor, no matter what level it was on. This would result in a longer ride in the lift than had been anticipated. It also lead to scenes of mild hysteria and mothers with young children riding up and down while trying desperately to get out of the building to do their shopping in the NAAFI van.

We had to wait six months before married quarters became available: not an easy time – having the three children sharing one bedroom and not having a washing machine. We moved into a married quarter at Easter 1968, but I was appointed deputy headmaster of Montgomery School, Hohne in September 1968 so we were on the move again - sorry to leave Osnabruck but delighted to become a deputy for the third time.

The Bergen Hohne Training Area was established in the southern part of the Luneberg Heath in 1935 as a military training area for the German Army. Twenty five villages and settlements were cleared so that the area could be used for tank ranges and exercises, artillery ranges and infantry training. Hohne garrison is a large barracks which contained a British Tank Regiment and Dutch Tank Regiment and a Royal Artillery Unit. Opposite the barracks is the village of Belen – which gave its name to the Bergen/Belsen concentration camp and remains today a memorial and documentation centre. The closest town of any size was Celle about 30kms away – but Hannover, Bremen and Hamburg were within reasonable distance. While waiting (again!) for a married quarter, I commuted to Osnabruck at weekends.

Montgomery School was a single-storey building with a large playing field alongside. The headmaster was most generous in involving me in all aspects of running the school – and putting me in charge of a class of seven year olds, which included his son. We enjoyed a number of excellent social functions, school concerts, a Year 6 week's camping on the ranges with the army's cooperation erecting our tents and cooking all our meals, two splendid Burns Night Suppers – with school halls, teachers & Officers Messes being the centre of our social activity.

Our home was in a two-storey barrack block converted into six flats, one of four such blocks surrounding a large central quadrangle of a field. The barrack blocks had previously accommodated the guards at the Belsen concentration camp. Unlike Dachau and Auschwitz where some original buildings or reconstructions give an immediate impact of what conditions were like, at Belsen my first impression was of nothing. Conditions were so unbelievably grim when the camp was liberated in 1945 that mass graves had to be dug for the ten thousand unburied bodies lying there, the living being immediately taken out to Hohne camp and Belsen burned to the ground. The entrance to Belsen, simply stating Bergen/Belsen 1940 to 1945 was included a documentation centre and a small museum. A far more informative and essential memorial and exhibition was completed in 1990.

Low stone walls now protect huge mounds of earth which in

season are covered in heather. Carved into the walls are the simplest and shocking inscriptions: *HierRuhe 2000* (here rest 2000), *HierRuhe 3000, HierRuhe 5000.* It is a place of uneasy silence and infinite sadness – and no birds sing.

We enjoyed one glorious summer and two freezing winters in Hohne and took advantage of our holiday opportunities – first camping and then caravanning in Spain and Italy, plus visits to Bremen, Hannover and Christmas markets in Hamburg.

It was only four terms before I was promoted again – to my first headship, which meant a return to Osnabruck.

Wellington School

Wellington School was the largest of the four primary schools in Osnabrück, the most spacious school I had seen. It overlooked two parade grounds and a full sized gymnasium. There was a small indoor swimming pool, garages, a small menagerie, a dining room, kitchen and a church.

My temporary home was the Officers' Mess of the King's Own Scottish Borderers, the school's "parent unit", responsible for supplies and materials. I was made a living-in member of the mess. We were roused from sleep by the sound of bagpipes outside the window. Unforgettable. On mess dinner nights the regimental silver was on display.

I knew most of the staff from my previous time in Osnabrück and I found I had more and more day to day interaction with parents than ever before, being involved closely with the school's parent unit and working with the other head teachers on the garrison.

Service Children's Schools work under conditions described

as 'turbulence'. The average tour of duty or 'posting' was two and a half years. We had four regiments in Osnabrück, each being posted in turn about every eighteen months. So up to a hundred or so children could depart, the new children arriving being of different age groups from the leavers. Careful reorganisation was vital. Sometimes servicemen were posted for a 3 month tour in Northern Ireland, leaving their families behind – the only stable family routine being school.

We enjoyed the German lifestyle – *Bratwurst* and *pommes frites* with mayonnaise at a *Schnellimbiss*, German beer and German wine; mulled wine at Christmas markets; Sunday walks in the woods followed by *Kaffee* and *Kuchen* and warmer Summers and colder Winters than we were used to.

School was never dull: class concerts and school productions, Garrison Schools concerts plus music and drama festivals, and athletic meetings with the primary schools in Münster. Staff development was a priority and we had visits and courses run by U.K. advisors, consultants and inspectors from the U.K. We had annual H.T. Conferences and I was flown occasionally to the UK. to join a panel of three (one Primary Head, one Secondary Head and an RAEC Officer) interviewing teachers.

While we spent our Christmases in Osnabrück, at Easter and in the summer we packed the car and caravan and headed for Southern climes and coasts. We explored Paris, Munich, Rome, Florence, Pisa, Innsbruck, Salzburg, Vienna, Lake Garda, Venice, the Cote d'Azur, southern Spain or the Adriatic coast. Half terms we stayed in Germany or just across the border in Holland.

The most dramatic drive was the one to Berlin, along the West-East corridor. We applied for permission to travel to Berlin through the school's parent unit. We received a document with a brightly coloured Union Jack giving our details, car registration and dates of travel written in English, French and Russian. The journey of about 140 km was to take between 2 ½ and 4 hours, with a speed limit of 50 kph. Start time would be notified to the RMP in Berlin:if you did the journey in less time you could be stopped by the East German Volkspolitzei (who you were *not* to stop or communicate with!). If you took longer than 4 hours the RMP would come out and look for you!

At the West German crossing point we were shown where to park by a Russian solder, entered a hut where passports were checked and documents stamped. We then proceeded along the Autobahn to which nothing appeared to have been done since the war. Heavily armed East German troops were in evidence at all checkpoints.

We did the sights –Reichstag, Brandenburg Gate, Zoo, Wannsee, Egyptian Museum in Charlottenburg and looked over the wall – we were able to use all military facilities such as the French Officers Club, the "*Pavilion du Lac*" where we had our first taste of snails and frogs legs. The US Army PX, the equivalent of our NAAFI, was an Aladdin's Cave of foodstuffs and goods – many of them new to us. Our first visit was a very full seven days of sightseeing and relaxing and we returned twice more before we finally left Germany.

Headmaster, Wellington School

Wellington School continued to grow in size and also in age-range. At the end of one day, only the deputy head, Keith Ingles, and I remained in the school. The 'phone rang and when I answered it, an Irish voice said, "There's a bomb in your school'. I ran into the cellar where Keith was collecting some exercise books. The cellar corridor was still packed with boxes and materials with one single central passageway. I told Keith about the phone call, he yelled out, "Jesus Christ", dropped the books he was carrying and I found that I was chasing *him* up the stairs to the nearest exit. I phoned the RMP who responded promptly but nothing was found.

At the conclusion of a Summer School in Wilhelmshaven one year, I learned that a new Middle School was to be built in each of our garrisons and we would have to retain our Year Seven children until the schools were built. He explained this would be for children from all four schools on the garrison and that the Station Officers' Mess would be converted during the holidays into an Annexe to accommodate them. I asked about extra staff only to be told, "I'm afraid you'll have to find them".

Everything worked out eventually and we now had a well converted 'annexe' with a science laboratory. It also worked to our family's advantage. Gaynor was now in Year 6 – so she was able to stay in Osnabrück for another 2 years before joining Alison in the Royal Latin School. They overlapped for only a short time for, after 'O' Levels, Alison wanted to come home and did her sixth form years commuting daily to Edinburgh School in Münster. Thirty years later, Alison returned to Münster as her husband was posted there. Edinburgh School was now the Dutch Army Barracks and where Alison returned to the 'School Hall' for social events over the three year posting.

The British Families Education Service became part of the worldwide Service Children's Education Authority, which did not regard itself as a "career service" so there could be no guarantee of service until the age of sixty or sixty-five. Staff could not remain beyond the age of fifty. Consequently teachers – particularly headteachers - began reading the appointments section of the *Times Educational Supplement* a few years before that deadline.

The new Middle School was soon too small and instead of taking our children from eight to twelve, we kept our eight year olds. I had a new young deputy headmaster – Gareth Morgans – and our son Gareth had started boarding school – Woolverstone Hall in Ipswich. Two of my Osnabrück colleagues (younger than me) had left for headships in England and I began to have 'Home Thoughts from Abroad" at the back of my mind.

I had kept in contact with Maurice Averill throughout my time in Germany and I was surprised when he wrote to say he was retiring: would I be interested in applying for the headship of Thorpe House School?. I phoned him, he invited me to come home one weekend for interview. I then applied, and was successful. .

We were returning home, back to the prep school sector.

Prep School Headmaster 1978-87

Having stepped on to the housing ladder we began to look at the options available to us. Unbelievably, at that time a couple of local estate agents advised us to sell our bungalow, because 'tenants didn't look after rented property'. Had we taken their advice we wouldn't have been able to afford to buy the same property when we returned to England. Ultimately we rented it fully furnished to the military base at nearby Beaconsfield Army School of Languages.

By Christmas 1978 we had settled into a four bedroom detached house in the village of Seer Green. Alison had begun college in High Wycombe (now Buckingham New University); Gaynor had transferred to Chesham High School; Gareth had returned to Woolverston Hall and Ray had taken up an appointment in one of the Junior forms in Thorpe House.

The main building and classrooms had a rather tired look about them. The boarding element had changed from full boarding to weekly boarding and Saturday morning lessons had been discontinued, and although there were some sporting fixtures and tournaments, there were no week-end duties for staff.

The school now owned its own playing fields: two rugby/soccer playing fields; a pavilion with changing rooms, showers, a kitchen and large room for 'match teas' and a bungalow presently occupied by the Second Master and his family. We were the only members of staff not accommodated by the school!

The school routine was well established. Kingscote with its own headmistress, was signposted as 'Kingscote Pre-Preparatory School for Thorpe House' and parents who applied for entry, or even a visit, came to me and I and introduced them to the Headmistress. We wanted to ensure continuity between the two schools.

Teachers in the Lower School stayed with the same classes while the specialist teachers in the Upper School were responsible for their own subjects and for their Common Entrance Examination results. It was all very comfortable. There were many good things being done. The games teachers were generous with their time after school hours. We had our own cub pack and scout troop, run by staff and parents which involved week-ends and summer camps, but some members of staff were contributing nothing outside the classroom while being well looked after by the school.

Staff accommodated in Heywood House were provided with breakfast, lunch (at the head of a table with the boys) and an evening meal seven days a week. I spoke to all the teachers who were not doing any extra-curricular activities and asked them if they were prepared to do so. I also pointed out that it would be a condition of employment for future members of staff. Fortunately they all agreed, one or two rather reluctantly – but we were able to offer a variety of after school clubs very quickly which were much appreciated by boys and parents.

It felt rather strange at first being in a much smaller, tighter school community and in a more formal setting, boys smartly turned out in school blazers and ties. They were expected to behave sensibly and work hard.

It was important to establish contact with Public School Headmasters and I began by visiting the schools where most of our boys were going – Merchant Taylors in Northwood, St.Edwards in Oxford, Aldenham, Bloxham, Pangbourne and Oundle. I was overwhelmed by the facilities and opportunities offered at the Public Schools. Such things the pupils of Porth Sec. in wartime days couldn't even dream of.

We received 'feed-back' on what our old boys were doing and invitations to come either to visit, with a small group of heads, or to functions of note in their school's history. I visited Eton, Harrow, Charterhouse, Stowe, Westminster, Wellington College, attended dinners at Merchant Taylor's Livery Hall and the Guildhall in London and participated in the Annual Conferences of the Incorporated Association of Preparatory Schools in Oxford & Cambridge University Colleges. A number of Public School Headmasters were guests of honour at the school's sports and prizegiving day. We also had the then secretary of the Amateur Athletics Association, Sir Michael Knight (Air Marshal and also a member of our RAF Akrotiri Rugby Team). My very first guest of honour was former Tonyrefail Grammar School boy, Cardiff, Wales & British Lions player & BBC Radio & Television Executive Cliff Morgan.

The school year has a pattern and a momentum of its own. A rugby term, a soccer term and a cricket/athletics and swimming term, parents evenings, school plays and concerts, ski trips and expeditions and end of term examinations in preparation for the Common Entrance Examination. Being located in Buckinghamshire, one of the last bastions of Grammar Schools, pupils were entered for the Secondary Selection tests at 'Eleven Plus' – the results of which deprived us of many potential scholars and had a considerable effect on the major games teams.

The 'Common Entrance' process itself was intriguing. The head office of IAPS sent out examination papers in English, Maths, Science, French, Latin, History, Geography and Scripture to all prep schools. The examinations took place on the same dates in all schools and individual scripts were sent directly to the candidates' first choice of public schools. The papers were marked internally by the school and the result sent back to the prep school who notified the parents of the results.

There were many aspects of my years in the independent sector which were most rewarding. I was particularly pleased with the wide variety of success the boys had achieved in so many fields. The school choir was well established; instrumental music had become integrated into the curriculum; boys had been involved in sailing, windsurfing, fencing, dry ski-ing and triathlons and some had achieved regional, county, national and even international success in badminton, tennis, squash, stamp collecting, BMX and archery.

It was however, the most difficult post in my teaching career. In theory the day-to-day running of the school was my responsibility but the maintenance and finance remained the province of Maurice Averill. He found it difficult to relinquish responsibility and a few long-serving members of staff by-passed me and went directly to him with any problems. In addition to which maintenance and upkeep of buildings, furniture and resources were minimal. It appeared that he was all in favour of progress as long as it didn't mean changing anything or involving any expenditure. A very supportive Parents & Old Boys Association provided our first computers, a school mini-bus and paid half the cost of a tennis court on the playing fields.

In July 1983 the Headmistress of Kingscote retired. Ray applied for the post and was appointed for September 1983

Then came the biggest change in the school's history – the school was to become a Charitable Trust instead of a family business. The new Board of Governors was formed by Maurice and the long, tedious process was completed in 1986. I felt that it was now time to move on.

This was going to require much thought and discussion because Ray was now well established as Headmistress of Kingscote.

Saudi Arabia 1987-96

We were both attracted by the idea of a last venture overseas. I applied for the headship of a British/Dutch school in Dharan, Saudi Arabia. It was policy to appoint only married couples to the District so Ray also was interviewed: I was appointed head (with a car included in the contract) and Ray was given a teaching post.

This was going to be a big move for us but we felt that the time was right

From the moment I landed at Dhahran International Airport, I was in a different world. Long, silent lines for passport inspection. Rigorous passport and customs inspections, most luggage opened for inspection, workers arriving with items of luggage tied with rope to have contents flung about and left to gather up. You were then free to enter—but not to leave the country. That meant applications to apply for an exit/re-entry visa through our Government Relations Saudi representative, and allow ten days for the process. Very different.

All male Saudi citizens wore men wore long, loose fitting white cotton robes, their heads covered by red and white check *ghutrahs* held in place by *agals*. The women were covered from neck to ankle in a loose fitting black dress (*abiyah*), heads covered by black scarves. Foreigners were also expected to dress modestly. Most women wore an *abiyah* over their western clothes, and I never saw a man wearing shorts in public. Fortunately, life inside Western "compounds" was far more relaxed and informal.

The only religion in the country was Islam. Prayer calls from the mosques came five times a day, shutters came down quickly on all shops and supermarkets and customers were quick to leave. During the Holy Month of Ramadan when Muslims fasted between sunrise and sunset, Westerners were careful not to be seen drinking from a water bottle, eating an ice cream or smoking in public. There were no theatres or cinemas or alcohol and women were not allowed to drive. It was a unique environment to be in but we found it to be interesting, often exciting, often amusing, but never dull.

A large number of staff came back to school well before the term began, for during the summer holidays the school furniture and equipment had been moved from its previous location to become part of the Dhahran Academy campus. Most of my problems in the first few days were devoted to dealing with staff whose materials weren't where they expected them to be and, later, with parents who were concerned about their children being transferred from a smaller, self-contained situation, plus a swimming pool to a vast campus with much older children – and no swimming pool!

In addition to the married couples "sponsored staff" mainly recruited from the United Kingdom and the United States, we relied on "locally engaged" staff – qualified teachers who were the wives of other Western employees. Ours came from ARAMCO (The Arabian/American Oil Company), KFUPM (The King Fahd University of Petroleum and Minerals) and BAE (British Aerospace).

We taught the children of more than thirty different nationalities, of every colour and creed – without any clashes of colour, culture or belief. They were all just children who made friends easily, enjoyed school and were a joy to teach. It made you wonder where it all goes wrong – perhaps living in narrow-minded 'ghettoes' instead of a complete mixture of cultures with no overwhelming majority and no national agendas.

The new challenge of working in a school on a large campus meant as school numbers changed, classrooms were exchanged from one school to another. We shared specialists in P.E, music, art and Arabic and the use of the large well-resourced Learning Resource Centre. There were also monthly meetings in Central Office with the headmaster from the outlying schools, shared in-service training with all teachers on the campus, plus two big conferences a year in the cities and countries we had never visited.

When Kuwait was invaded by Saddam Hussein on August 2nd school staff were scattered around the world on holiday and the official instruction we were given was to "sit and wait." News kept coming through on radio and TV and living conditions in Saudi Arabia were shown in a poor light—sand and desert. Administrative staff were recalled at the end of August, and those teachers who wished to return were advised to do so in September. The Board of Trustees anticipated lower numbers of children arriving so offered unpaid leave to those teachers who wished to remain in the UK or USA.

We then entered a phony war period with armed personnel appearing in numbers in the streets, a build-up of men and materials and when men started arriving from their desert locations a scheme was launched—Scrub a Squaddie—to entertain troops (usually American) and give them a chance of a hot shower and civilised amenities. Then on January 17th I was awoken at 3 am to be told that we were bombing Baghdad and advised to put our emergency systems in operation. It was the first of many such calls, as we heard the sound of Patriot missiles being launched to intercept incoming Scud missiles and staff and children were issued with gas masks. For me it brought back memories of my childhood in the Rhondda in 1940.

Ray and I left to spend a weekend in Bahrain on February 27th and woke up next day to hear that the "hundred days war" was over. In celebration we attended the Bahrain Welsh Society's annual St David's Day dinner that evening—and "everyone burst out singing".

We had managed to maintain a calm and stable manner at the school during those tense days: for many children familiar school routines were the only stable thing in an unstable world.

Once things had settled down life returned to normal. The Association of Near East/South Asia Schools, based in Athens organised two major staff development conferences a year: the second conference which coincided with our schools' Spring Break was for all Administrators and teachers – from over one hundred schools. They were followed by a few free days of exploration: Istanbul, Athens, Cairo, New Delhi, Kuala Lumpur, Colombo, Nairobi, Rome. During my final years I also attended the ever larger annual conference of the European Council of International Schools in Nice, Hamburg & the Hague.

I also accompanied the Director of Personnel to the European Council of International Schools' Annual Recruiting Fair in London to interview teachers for both British Schools. During the Gulf War, which inevitably was a time of great tension in the area, Ray travelled with me to London in case the District's evacuation plan had to be put into operation. And that was precisely when a mortar was fired at Downing Street! I was also charged with organising a conference in London – four days at the London Hilton in Park Lane.

Ray and I visited Bahrain regularly, drove to Jeddah and Yanbu and snorkelled in the Red Sea, drove to Dubai and flew to Muscat, visited Jordan, Petra and Wadi Rum, the Crusader castles, and spent a few days in Damascus. What a splendid take-off platform Saudi Arabia was for exploring the surrounding countries.

And there was a meeting with Royalty. In 1992, the Prince of

Wales visited the Eastern Province and I met him with other staff and fifty pupils while as Secretary of the British Businessmen's Association I was invited to dinner and the beating of the retreat on H.M.Y Brittania in Dammam Port. In chatting to Prince Charles I informed him that during the same week that I was meeting him, my eldest daughter was meeting the Queen who was visiting Army Garrisons in Germany. The first time in British history when the monarch and heir to the throne had met with two members of the Brunt family!

We spent Christmas in our last year in Saudi in Damascus; our last day in Al Khabar where a bomb exploded close by in a block of flats occupied by American servicemen—too close to the school for comfort.

The Last Hurrah

I finally retired in 1996. I had assumed retirement meant just that and we had begun to settle into a life of scraping ice off car windows, taking trips to London theatres, gardening, watching rugby, spending time with children and grandchildren, and suffering a "welcome home" burglary. But it seemed my professional life was not yet over. A fledgling international school in Tallin, Estonia was in difficulty and an experienced head and teacher were required urgently, for January 1997. Were we interested?

So we soon found ourselves in the ice and snow of Tallin.

The city is a lovely, walled, cobblestoned capital: one of the best preserved mediaeval cities in Europe, with its fortified upper town, housing the Estonian Parliament and a Russian Orthodox Cathedral, while the lower town is a tangle of streets and alleyways and alcoves where traders sold their wares. But the contrast between a Saudi summer and Estonian winter was dramatic winter days were so dark it was almost like working underground in the Rhondda! But Spring arrived almost in an instant, to be celebrated with the annual Singing Festival and a dance festival in May.

We took the opportunity to visit Helsinki, Riga, Stockholm and St Petersberg while we worked at establishing the school on a sound footing and procure new premises with large classrooms, a gymnasium, dining room and large outside play area. The board asked us to extend our contract but we declined and at our farewell lunch were were joined by the ambassadors for Norway, Russia and Germany with their wives.

It was time to retire…again.

Not that our final retirement proved to be a house-bound one. Over the last twenty years we have been able to visit our son in Canada on several occasions, there have been regular annual cruises to exotic locations such as the Canary Islands and Madeira, the Caribbean and Florida, as well as visits to Alaska and South Africa, Australia and the Pacific islands Crete, Bilbao, Krakow, Vienna, Prague and Budapest…and the Millennium Stadium to support Wales—even though I don't really understand the modern game!

I was still called upon professionally in 2000, for international school accreditation visits, to Rotterdam and Kuwait and of course there have been family weddings, great grandchildren have arrived, we received a card from the Queen to congratulate us on our Diamond Wedding Anniversary and we've been able to enjoy numerous visits to London theatres.

Just over a year ago I visited Cardiff to meet Dewi Griffiths who took me on a trip down memory lane. It was a glorious Summer day and I was stunned to see, "How Green is my Valley now". It looked lovelier than it ever did when the pit wheels were turning; when the time was recorded by the sound of the pit hooters at the end of a shift; and when the rivers of the Rhondda and the Taff ran coal black. But driving along the streets, shops were closed and shuttered, pubs closed or used for other purposes, gaps in the landscape where chapels once stood or, worse, chapels held up by scaffolding. There was a feeling of decay. The vibrant feel good optimism had gone. It was a day of very mixed emotions.

Although I am still proud to have spent my formative years in the Rhondda, I have no regrets about leaving. It is ironic that the Grammar Schools which enabled so many children to gain the basic qualifications for higher education and to enter the professions were also responsible for robbing the valleys of many of their brightest assets.

On leaving school, I am also thankful for my two 'gap years' of National Service before going to college and the 'university of life' experiences that they provided.

In choosing a career in teaching I was merely travelling on the conveyor belt of that time in the belief that teaching was a noble profession, a 'clean job' and a lifetime occupation. There were no 'careers advisers' in schools then. It was a career that I loved and I look back with great pleasure and for the opportunities it gave me and later, the family, to travel and to experience more than I could ever have imagined doing. Teaching was also a source of great fun and enjoyments.

Family life has been the greatest gift of all. We now have three ('middle-aged') children, six grandchildren and two great-grandchildren – a close-knit family unit.

Since 1953 the constant in my life has been Ray. We have done so much together and celebrated our Diamond Wedding Anniversary in 2015. Many people describe their closest and dearest as their 'Rock'. On the contrary, Ray's love, wisdom, common-sense and strength have made her the pilot and navigator who has kept me clear of the rocks and I would have achieved nothing without her.

Not exactly formal attire!

AFTERWORD

There are some who are mentioned in this volume who have been unable to present their own accounts of their childhood and careers.

Roy Lewis writes: "It was Keith Lewis who drew me into the group of friends in 1947. His mother had died young, his father had remarried and he was brought up by his grandmother Mrs Connelly in Kennard Street. He was athletic: he ran the mile at school, was the boldest and bravest of cyclists in our group, but it was rugby that was his first love. He played for Porth County and persuaded me to join him at Treorchy Rugby Club. His usual position was at wing-forward but he was also handy at centre three-quarter. I played alongside him in the centre against Cardiff Boys Club and scored 4 tries, courtesy of his bludgeoning runs inside me. I never achieved such a feat again. He also brought school friend Brian Roberts into the group. Brian, a self-admittedly libidinous character as a young man, nevertheless had an unblemished career as a teacher in Market Harborough before his retirement, after two marriages, to Wales. He was unable to play rugby since as a child he had received a pellet in his eye from a recklessly discharged airgun. It was deemed too close to his brain to be removed, and remains there to this day.

Brian and I were somewhat miffed when Keith gave up our evening excursions in the 1950s. We put it down to marital pressure, after he married Avril Owen from Kenry Street in

Tonypandy. In fact his reluctance was due to his working evenings at the correspondence course to become a mine surveyor. Keith became a member of the Royal Institute of Chartered Surveyors after an apprenticeship underground, and in later life was a director of the Housing Corporation of Wales. He would have experienced considerable pride when his son became a qualified architect.

As for the lottery of the 11+ it can be exemplified by the case of Ceridwen Thomas. A bright girl, she did well and went to Porth County. She entered accountancy after school and went on to Cambridge, but her husband had had difficulty passing the 11+ in Cathays High School in Cardiff. Nevertheless he also went to Cambridge, became a doctor and together they forged careers in the United States.

Longevity brings its sadnesses, of course. Keith Lewis has gone, as has Buck Evans and Lem Evans, Enid Benbow, Marilyn Davies and Josie Morris. Roy Wynne and Gareth Griffiths passed away recently. At Bristol University I had played with Graham Powell in the centre, while my scrum-half was Tony O'Connor: both Graham and Tony passed away in their early eighties.

Meanwhile, I suppose the rest of us are tottering towards senility!"

Dewi Griffiths has memories of Mansel Lloyd. "Mansel, like me, joined the BBC and became a well respected editor, working with Cliff Michelmore on the *Tonight* programme. His career continued with his work on current affairs programmes such as, *Midweek, 24 Hours,* and *Nationwide* during the period

1962-76. He also worked in Yorkshire Television for a while."

Leighton Brunt also recalls Mansel: "Mansel's father was the caretaker and cleaner of Bethesda Chapel so we had access to the chapel throughout the week, able to use the Sunday School classrooms upstairs - or the Chapel itself. Mansel, like Tom Sawyer who persuaded boys to pay an apple for the privilege of painting his fence, encouraged us to help his father to clean the Chapel. The two aisles, leading from the rear, and main entrance of the Chapel, and the pulpit had wooden block floors. We polished the floors by dropping dollops of polish, tied rags over our shoes and 'skated' down the sloping aisles one behind the other - with some difficulty at first, but most enjoyable after a few 'runs'".

Another Gelli and Pentre Sec boy who did well in his career was Keith Slade, *Gwyn Evans comments*. "Born in 1930 Keith had the uplifting experience during the war of acquiring a "brother": his mother took in a Jewish refugee, Erich Bluh. Erich attended Bronllwyn School where his ability went unnoticed and he worked at a bakery in Treorchy after school. He returned to Vienna after the war and learned that his parents had died in Auschwitz, so he came back to England and remained a close friend of Keith's.

Keith still recalls the smell of wet clothing in the classrooms of those days: satchels and coats were hung on radiators to dry. And in 1942 his mother was informed that Keith's father had been interned by the Japanese: it blighted family life. After school he was commissioned while on National Service at Brecon and on his release he attended St Paul's, Cheltenham (working part time at Tongwynlais where Dewi Griffiths now lives) and then obtained a post as Housemaster at a Devon school, while contemplating a career in the Army. The school, Bradfield, was an Elizabethan pile and his room was off the minstrel's gallery. Quite a change from a terraced house in Gelli!

Keith married the nursing sister at the school and after six years was appointed to the West of England School (the blind school) at Exeter. There he remained for the next thirty years, finally becoming headmaster. After a visit by John Major, the then Prime Minister wrote *"Having seen the school for myself I m not in the least surprised that you have an international reputation which attracts people from all over the world to learn from your methods. Thank you also for the Braille message which will always remind me of an outstanding school."*

Subsequent to that visit, Keith was awarded an OBE. He had another claim to fame: he was once arrested at a motorway café, on suspicion that he was the missing Lord Lucan! He now lives quietly in a National Trust property in Devon."

The Workmens Institute 1950